©2018 Rod Whitlock

Design - James Gerhold

Editor - Scott Firestone IV

Ordering Information:

Special discounts are available on quantity purchases. For details, contact Rod at Rod@RodWhitlock.com.

www.RodWhitlock.com

ISBN: 978-1981952960

Printed in the United States of America.

Rod Whitlock

ABANDONED

Dedication

This is my story.

A story that took me over 50 years to write. *Abandoned* is full of personal stories from over those years, about the people who have helped shape my life and this book. This book describes the many encounters that deeply influenced my life, and expresses gratitude to friends who remain true friends to this day. So it goes without saying that there's no way to list the multitudes of people who have had a life-altering impact on my life.

I do want to begin by thanking my Lord and Savior, Jesus. He took a discarded life and brought hope through His shocking display of love, extreme mercy, and outrageous grace. My transformation has demanded extreme patience on His part. Yet He remained by my side during the revolution. His grace challenges me to live a more courageous life for Him.

I also wish to thank my mom. You stayed when others abandoned me. You could have easily discarded me but you chose the more difficult path of raising a boy as a single mom. You did all of this while also living a life of rejection.

To my wife, Kim, thank you for believing in me and sticking by my side for the past 33 years. I can't think of anyone else I'd rather do life with than you. I couldn't have asked for a more loving, faithful, patient, and understanding wife. You're really pretty, too.

Thank you to my kids Lindsay, Bethany, Michael, and Christopher. You choose to love me and embrace me as your daddy, amidst all my shortcomings. Your love has helped me make it through many days of my life. I treasure those days when your smile, text, hug, or laughter at my "dad joke" reminded me that love still exists and has knocked on the door of my heart. It's more than a cliché when I say, "You have saved my life."

To the new additions to my world: my sons-in-love Kyle and Griffin, and daughter-in-love Micaela. I look forward to each time we're able to spend time together. I enjoy the diversity of gifts and personality you bring to the family and to my life. You remind me that my purpose on earth goes beyond the borders of my past, the limitation of my failures, or the confines of my abilities.

I also wish to dedicate this book to each and every friend and momentary acquaintance along my travels. You made my journey more memorable. Some of you have walked with me for years, and others for just a brief moment in time along my stretch of road. I'm grateful for both experiences for different reasons. You've been a pool of refreshing, cool water during those hot, sweltering days when life had me in the wilderness of insecurity.

Finally, I dedicate this work to each individual who has encountered the pain of abandonment. My prayer is that as you read the following pages the hopes and dreams within you are resurrected. May God, our Father, transform and restore your lives, renewing greater purpose and meaning.

Introduction

Finish reading the story God is still writing.

"Jesus also did many other things. If they were all written down, I suppose the whole world could not contain the books that would be written" (John 21:25).

The Bible is filled with stories about people. In reality it's a story about God and His love for people. Over the next several pages you'll read stories about my life growing up with four fathers. Truth be told, however, it's more accurate to say it's a story about one Father—a Father who committed Himself to me in the midst of continual abandonment.

In no way have I included every story. Rather, my attempt was to include stories that divulge the hurt in my life, and how a loving God cared for me through that pain. For this reason, the stories you read aren't in chronological order. Instead, I've written them around themes of God's outrageous grace operating in my life.

"I knew you before I formed you in your mother's womb. Before you were born I set you apart and appointed you as my prophet to the nations" Jeremiah 1:5.

It was a Sunday morning in 1981. I was 19 years old. My pastor, Sam Mayo, introduced the guest speaker for the morning message. Don't ask me who he was or what he spoke on. I don't remember. The one thing I do recall was the conversation following the service. I'd made my way up to the front in order to spend some time in prayer.

I knelt down, resting my elbows on the blue-carpeted altar bench. After a few moments of talking with Jesus, I felt a hand gently come to rest on my head. It was the speaker. He was praying for me. Following his prayer he moved on to pray with others. A few minutes later I stood to my feet, making my way toward the exit, but the speaker approached me.

God was giving him a prophetic message that would have life-altering ramifications for the rest of my life.

"I believe God is going to use your life story to bring hope and healing to many people," he said.

Up to this point we had never met. I'm not even sure he asked me my name. He spoke those words, followed by a short prayer, and walked away. I never saw him again.

Each one of us is on a journey, with a tale to tell. Our life story isn't really an account about us; rather, it's a narrative about God. That morning, the plot of mine changed. My storyline was being transformed.

Outrageous grace.

It's about moving from being deserted to living a life of abandonment. It's a tale of how God worked through the pain of my past in order to give me a purpose in my present. He wishes to do the same in your life.

In all honesty I really never thought anyone would be interested in reading a book about my life. If I believed anything that day it was that the minister had grabbed the wrong guy. I didn't have anything to offer.

The testimonies of life-change in those days were of individuals being set free from sex, drugs, and rock-n-roll. I was none of those things, and therefore thought I had nothing to offer. I was a pretty good kid—excelled in school, active in sports, home by my curfew, took out the trash, etc… How was God going to use this?

Over the course of my life I've had countless people encourage me to pen this for others to read. At times, and as crazy as it sounds, people I've just met have encouraged me as well. Initially I dismissed the requests as nothing more than people being nice. I assumed they simply felt horrible for me, and this was their way of making me feel valued. Over time, however, the request seemed to grow stronger. To not do so would render me gravely disobedient.

My journey with Jesus has taught me that God echoes. In other words, He continually speaks the same message to us as a way to confirm it's Him speaking. So it is that the book you hold in your hand is a result of nothing more than my hearing God echo.

My life begins with a dad who abandoned me, followed by one who was assassinated, and later a dad who was alcoholic and abusive, and finally one who was caught in adultery. As a result, many of the names in this book have been changed to protect their identity and their extended families.

In no way is what you hold in your hand meant to bring blame, harm, revenge, or pain to any individual. It isn't a book about them. Rather, it's a story about my heavenly Father and how He never left me. He has been faithful through each raging storm, deep valley, and painful memory. He is a Healer, Comforter, Father, and so much more!

So it is that I invite you to read my story—or should I say an account—of God's tremendous love and outrageous grace for a young boy in search of a father.

Contents

ABANDONED

ROD WHITLOCK

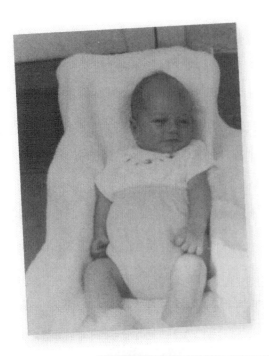

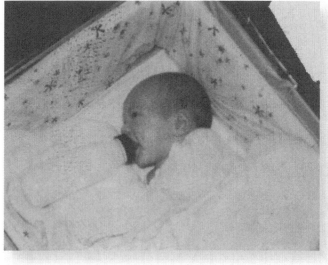

CHAPTER ONE

...AND THEY LIVED HAPPILY EVER AFTER?

Your past is about how you got here. Your future is about what you're going to do now that you are here

In May of 2010 I found myself on a ministry trip to Oakland, California. We had gathered in the office of the president of one of our Bible schools. After a few moments of prayer he began to speak prophetically into my life. A few days later he would email me the message God had placed on his heart.

"As we prayed in my office, this is what I saw: a rustic house (possibly a log cabin) built in the deep woods on a mountain slope. Beside the house was a stream with rushing waters flowing down the mountain through the deep woods. There seemed to be no other houses around. As I watched you approach the stream, I noticed it was so loud that nothing else could be heard—no insects, people, animals, and all the usual things you hear in the woods. God said to tell you that the closer you get to the stream, the more he will break off of your life the voices of failure, inadequacy, and never-quite-measuring-up. It's in the voice of the rushing waters, His Holy Spirit, that defines who you are and the boundaries for your life, family, and ministry. No man can define that for you.

" *'The voice of the Lord is upon the waters...The voice of the Lord is powerful, The voice of the Lord is majestic. The voice of the Lord breaks the cedars...The voice of the Lord hews out flames of fire. The voice of the Lord shakes the wilderness...The Lord sat as King at the flood; Yes, the Lord sits as King forever. The Lord will give strength to His people; the Lord will bless His people with peace" (Psalm 29:3-5, 7-11 NASB).'*

"Be blessed and encouraged my friend. God loves you and has a perfect plan for your life!"

The book you now hold in your hand is my journey to discover that stream in the woods.

We all have a story. Mine began in sunny California, during the summer of 1961. John F. Kennedy was president and the Yankees would go on to win the World Series. Fred Flintstone would utter the words, "Yabba Dabba Doo!" on television sets across the country. Mankind reached space for the first time. It was also the year a dividing wall went up, separating West Berlin from East Berlin and East Germany. The Berlin Wall was a massive structure, one that often separated families, and began a new and dark chapter in the history of our world. A barrier separating families was, for many, a physical reminder of how the enemy of our souls works. Though his ways are much more subtle, he works overtime to obliterate families, leaving behind forsaken individuals seemingly trapped on the other side of the barricade.

My blockade first displayed itself in the summer of '61, on a pre-arranged blind date—a meeting that would change the future for a couple of teenagers. Lynda and Rod had graduated high school the year before, and after graduating, Rod dutifully enlisted in the military.

Although Rod and Lynda had never met before, they had mutual friends in Ed and Margaret. It would be these shared friends who would introduce Rod and Lynda to one another for the first time. The four of them embarked on a double date—a rendezvous that would alter their lives. Ed and Margaret were convinced this would be a match made in heaven for the young couple.

Rod's first sighting of this attractive young woman came on a cool California evening, with the ocean waves hugging the sands of the Golden

State. As he laid eyes on Lynda, Rod's heart must have crashed as hard against the walls of his chest as the waves crashed against the beach. At least, this is how I like to imagine it taking place. We all dream that the people responsible for our arrival on this big blue ball were wholly faithful to each other "'til death do them part." Unfortunately, life doesn't always have a "they lived happily ever after" ending.

Lynda was a 5'5", attractive, 19-year-old brunette who would soon leave the teenage years in her rearview mirror. Sadly, her early years as a child left her scarred with extreme physical, emotional, and sexual abuse. Years of excessive mistreatment, severe neglect, and continual rejection had taken its toll on her spiritually, emotionally, physically, and mentally. On the outside, Lynda was a beautiful cheerleader and volleyball player, but on the inside she was confused and injured.

As a young child, Lynda was callously locked in a closet without so much as a slice of bread, a drop of water, or an appropriate bathroom option—all for no reason. Throughout her upbringing she was regularly denied basic hygiene that you and I take for granted. This ugly neglect displayed itself later in her life. At the young age of 30, Lynda had to have all but six teeth pulled, causing her to need dentures. This painful procedure came as a result of her mom keeping her from brushing her teeth as a youngster. Now 19, Lynda embraced living on her own, away from the family that tormented her. She could finally live the life she had only dreamed about while watching movies or reading a glamour magazine. She was free to do as she wished, with whom she desired, where and how she wanted.

Her blind date, Rod, had recently joined the military and received his first assignment along the coast of Northern California. This one-in-a-million coincidental meeting would forever change the trajectory of two lives, along with the stories they would choose to tell or keep a secret.

Ed and Margaret were dating at the time, too, and would eventually go on to get married. That marriage would literally last a lifetime, as Ed's death over 30 years later was the only thing that could separate them. This was quite a contrast to the eventual outcome of the "match-made-in-heaven" couple they'd set up.

The stage was now set. As the sun set on this July evening, the two 19-year-old men stepped aside from the ladies to make a crude wager. A five-dollar bet. Rod bet Ed that he would be able to have sex with Lynda before the sun said good night over the waters of the Pacific. Ed confidently agreed to the stakes, assured it would be one he couldn't lose. After all, it was a first date and the morals of the early '60s didn't lend themselves to this type of first-date behavior. An easy five bucks, he thought.

As the temperature dropped along the coast and the evening sun crawled down the western skies, the five-dollar bill moved from Ed's hand to Rod's pocket. Rod had "won." The outcome? Rod found himself a little richer. Lynda found herself pregnant.

Being a single mom in the early '60s was taboo, to say the least. To have sex outside of marriage and wind up carrying a child was viewed very differently than it is today. Today's culture suggests that a single woman getting pregnant is some type of merit badge, and even celebrated in some circles. But that wasn't the case with my mom. Yet, amid social pressure and degrading remarks from extremely abusive family members, she made the best decision of her life and mine, deciding to carrying me the entire nine months. It was during this same nine-month period that my dad departed, leaving behind a single mom and abandoning his soon-to-be-born baby boy. Abandonment is only one aspect of the story, and was the first voice to drown out the sound of the rushing stream in the woods.

So it was that on March 31, 1962, just minutes before April 1, I was born and introduced to a now-20-year-old single mom. My mom later told me that the doctor asked her if she was willing to wait another 13 minutes to have an April Fool's baby, to which she replied, "Get this baby out of me now!"

I was born in the same city where that college president spoke the prophetic word to me: Oakland, California. Coincidence? Not at all. God was silencing the voices of the enemy in my life.

Before leaving the hospital my mom named her blonde, blue-eyed baby boy after her boyfriend and my biological father. His name would be the only information I'd ever have about my dad.

I've never seen or met my biological father. I don't know if he's alive today, married, or has other children. I'll never know how long he spent in the military, which military bases he was assigned to, or what rank he obtained. I never heard him say, "I love you" or "I'm proud of you" or "Take out the trash!" There will never be a father/son talk over Saturday morning cereal, a favorite "guy movie," or burger and shake lunch the two of us will share. There will never be any pictures of the two of us playing catch, or home movies of him teaching me how to ride a bike or taking me fishing. No one will ever hear me tell the story of how he tucked me in at night, read me a bedtime story, or kissed my forehead before he shut the lights off. Neither will there be any spoiling from his parents, my grandparents. There are a million more "nevers" I can only imagine and will never realize.

Sadly, all too many of you reading this have experienced the pain and emptiness of abandonment that leads to the "nevers" in life. Perhaps your story is tragically similar to mine. Maybe you've had a father leave you, or even both parents leave—parents who abandoned you for no reason, or a senseless one. Maybe your story includes the struggle and agony of abuse.

I've met people who had both parents remain in their lives, but they were absent emotionally. For others, the face of abandonment looks like a spouse or a close friend leaving you. Regardless, the aching and reality of rejection changes the game of life for far too many people. The road of abandonment is cluttered with shattered promises, painful memories, and broken people.

Fortunately, my mother not only stayed with me but also continued to love and care for me. This wasn't always an easy task for a young, single mom of 20, without the support of family members. Couple this with the cultural stigma surrounding a single mom in the early '60s, and you can imagine the awful whispers behind her back. Still, she managed to raise her son, (a good-looking one, I might add), with little backing from family or others. After her childhood, she was used to doing without the life-sustaining care we all need. Having a child would now change the game—she would do her best to ignore her own pain, and choose to show the world she could properly care for a child.

About 19 years after my illegitimate birth, I found myself at Ed and Margaret's Midwest home. My mom had gotten married, and at the start of my ninth-grade year of school, thanks to a military transfer, our family was now stationed near Ed and Margaret's home. Four years later, following my high school graduation, my parents and siblings were transferred to England, but I remained behind to attend college at the University of Nebraska.

Ed and Margaret had been married for several years at this point, and had adopted two children of their own, as they were never able to have children. I find it sadly ironic that the couple who were married and stayed together were unable to have children, but a one-night-stand between two teenagers brought about an illegitimate son.

With my family in England, I would travel back to Omaha on the weekends in order to attend church. During the weekends I was able to stay with Ed and his family, and one warm spring evening Ed and I were sitting on the front porch of his home. We sat there talking about sports, school, food, and guy stuff, when he asked a question that changed everything.

"Did you know that your mom and dad weren't married?" Ed inquired, not knowing if this had been shared with me.

I sat silent, curiously staring at him.

My mom had always told me that she and my biological dad had once been married.

Ed told me about the blind date, the five-dollar bet, and how the relationship had ended shortly after my mom discovered she was pregnant.

CHAPTER TWO

LIFE FROM THE BACK OF A STATION WAGON

"If you want a happy ending, that depends, of course, on where you stop your story." –Orson Welles

"Even if my father and mother abandon me, the Lord will hold me close" (Psalm 27:10).

Following my near-miss, April Fool's Day birth, my mom found herself in a relationship with another man. Like my biological father, he was also a military man. The two were married, and in January of 1964, my half-brother was born. Just as with her relationship with my biological father, this one didn't last very long. And, just as with my father, I don't know much regarding my second dad. This difference in this short-lived relationship is that it ended in divorce. My mom now faced raising two young boys as a single 23-year-old.

Life has a way of throwing a curve-ball at us when we least expect it. It certainly did for my mom.

Don't get me wrong. My mom made some foolish decisions that led to painful, life-altering consequences. Our lives aren't always a result of the harshness brought on by others, or the unfairness of life. Often it's our own undoing that leads to a life filled with grief, regret, and sorrow. With heartache being her only constant companion, soon my mom found herself married for the second time. Once again, it was a military man, and she was soon pregnant with her third child. This time she would deliver a baby girl, a half-sister to my brother and me. Now our family consisted of three siblings—all with different fathers.

Perhaps having a girl would alleviate much of the sadness my mom had suffered while *she* was a little girl. It's possible the sounds of a girl, all dressed up and skipping through the house or playing with an assortment of dolls, would bring her the joy that life had robbed from her. This was a chance to turn her life around and raise a girl the way little girls were supposed to be raised: nurtured. Never locked in any closet, rather, her child would have opportunities to happily bounce into a closet to find a princess dress and shoes like the ones Cinderella wore to the ball. My mother loved her boys, but her girl would bring closure to her past. A daughter would mark the beginnings of her own fairytale ending—a carriage pulled by beautiful white horses and a "happily ever after." Regrettably, midnight was once again approaching, turning the carriage and horses back into reality for my mom and our dysfunctional home.

The serpent of abandonment has a way of slithering into houses and hearts. Our enemy is bent on destroying lives and separating families, and finds great delight in doing so. My mom had survived three fathers and five mothers, and this doesn't include the people her fathers and mothers were married to prior to entering her life, or once they left her. You could say my family tree looks more like an orchard linked with other orchards. Sadly, much of the fruit from those orchards has been marred through extreme neglect. The front entrance of her residence was more like a revolving door. The abandonment serpent appears in a multitude of ways…

- Men constantly coming and going
- Abusive parents
- Step-siblings
- New neighborhoods
- New schools

- Distant friends
- Rejection
- Shame
- Loneliness
- Scars
- Countless tears
- More abandonment

With each new parent, or new move, this ugly monster grew substantially stronger in her life—it commanded more of her emotions and claimed more of her tender heart. Surely, once she moved out on her own she'd be able to find sincere love and begin to live the life she always dreamed of as a little girl.

Just a year and a half later, my mom was married for the second time, and was welcoming a fourth child—her second little girl. Unfortunately, this marriage lasted only a few years longer than the previous one. Before my ninth birthday, my third dad had made his way through the family revolving door. I was left confounded, seeing yet another man enter our home, and then depart as if it was normal for this to happen to little boys.

It's hard to convey how much this affected me. Men came into our home for a moment, and then left without a trace—men who carried their own emotional baggage, filled with hurts and damaged ideas. I would wake one morning and not have a dad anymore. Another day I would be introduced to a new dad. I was never told why certain dads would leave and other ones would appear. Honestly, I didn't know if it was right to even ask that question.

Each new dad was simply the equivalent of getting a new television set: nice to look at for a while, until mom changed the channel. Each time I met a new man, I wondered if I was meeting a new dad. I suppose after going through a few, I didn't care. New half-siblings would appear and stay, new homes would come and go, and new schools were a constant part of my story. Life was embarrassingly awkward at times as I tried to make sense of it all.

There were a few bright spots growing up. Between the ages of five and eight, my half-brother and I spent summers visiting his grandparents in Mississippi. Riding the tractor on the 300-acre farm, fishing in one of the many ponds for catfish and bass, and shooting my grandpa's .22 were fond boyhood memories. But these joyful recollections battled against my unstable childhood. I was on one of life's roller coasters. The problem was I didn't really know if these were my memories or my brother's—after all, these were his grandparents, not mine. As much as I enjoyed the summers we spent in Mississippi, they only served to remind me that I didn't really belong anywhere.

My step-brother's dad, my mom's second husband, was married again with his own kids, and lived near my brother's grandparents. Some hot summer days I would see him and his family, and I remember the confusion I had over whether or not to call him dad, or by his first name, or…well, I didn't really call him anything. I would just start talking, hoping he knew I was speaking to him. Even as a young boy I remember being able to engage in conversations with someone as if I totally belonged, when in actuality I was only trying to survive.

As a result, humor became a trustworthy companion of mine. Making others laugh was a way for me to feel accepted in an otherwise unaccepting environment. I found that getting a laugh from others meant they were now listening to me, and I wouldn't have to gain their attention.

In addition to spending summers on the farm, I recall spending Sundays in the quaint, painted-white Baptist church in the small town near the farm. My step-grandparents were very religious and we never missed church on Sunday. It was my first, short-lived experience attending church and hearing about God. Our home life didn't include Sunday church gatherings. Though we attended each Sunday through the summer, I don't remember much about God or church. What I do remember is sitting up as tall as possible so I could watch the choir. Not that I enjoyed listening to hymns as a boy, but I was completely captivated by one of the prettiest girls I'd ever seen in my life. She was simply angelic. I didn't mind going to church at all!

As wonderful as summers in Mississippi were, they also proved to be somewhat confusing. For example, one summer my brother and I flew to our new home in Arizona, only to find our mom with another man. They weren't married at this point. What made this even more puzzling was that the prior summer my mom and then-third dad drove from New Mexico to Mississippi to bring us back home. This was due to the fact that my brother's grandparents wanted to keep my step-brother. I'm not sure they wanted me in that deal. The two summers meant back-to-back trips visiting my step-brother's grandparents in Mississippi. I was spending one school year in New Mexico and one in Arizona. This also meant three different dads. One in New Mexico, one in Mississippi, and a third in Arizona. I understand if things are a bit cloudy.

This took place during my time with my third set of grandparents, my step-sister's grandparents. We lived just down the street from them in New Mexico and would spend Saturday mornings at their house. So it was that I visited two dads, neither of which were my dads, spent time with two sets of grandparents, neither of which I could fully embrace as mine, while living in a home with a step-dad, a half-brother, and two half-sisters. We may have had a dog or cat, too. As I type this, it doesn't really make much sense *now*, so I can only imagine the emotions circling my head as a young boy. I didn't live in a home with family. I existed in a dwelling with people.

When I was in third grade, following my mom's second divorce, from my third dad, my mom once again found herself in love with another man. She announced she was getting married—her third wedding, ushering in my fourth dad. All of those verses in the Bible that talk about our forefathers? I totally understand what they're talking about!

With a new dad came a fresh location. We settled in Paradise Valley, Arizona. The three things I knew about our new dad were his name, that he was also a military man (along with my other three dads), and that he drove a 1970 Corvette. I mention his Corvette because, while this dad was just another dad, I'd never had one with such a nice car. I was smitten with that car more than I was with him.

You can easily understand my struggles with my own identity and value. I didn't belong to anyone. I didn't know where to call home. And I really had no family, although I was surrounded by step-siblings, step-grandparents, or step-dads. I was emotionally disconnected. Though I didn't realize it at the time, looking back I understand how my own personal values came into being. I began to value things over people. My fourth dad's Corvette had more of my heart than any member of the family.

I've heard it said that the most formative years in the life of a child are during the first six years of life. According to those who study this, the emotions I'd experienced up to this point had the potential of forever shaping my thinking, lifestyle choices, and outlook on life. Thankfully, I would finally meet a man who would forever help re-shape those emotions, wounds, and erratic thinking patterns. But I'm getting ahead of myself.

Believe it or not, the six of us would all pile in to the '70 'Vette whenever we travelled together as a family. Of course, this was before seatbelt laws, child seats, or common sense. But like many families today, you adapt to the situation and do what you have to do in order to make it through life. Shortly thereafter, my parents traded the 'Vette for a station wagon. If this wasn't love, I'm not sure what was. This swap proved to be a roomier, but far less cool, mode of transportation for a family of six. I do recall riding with my step-brother in the far back seat, which faced backwards. We were able to see everything behind us— where we'd been and how far we'd come.

Finally we were a family! We had another dad, a fresh house, a different location, and a new car. Funny how we go through life believing that new somehow means better. Don't get me wrong. Things were definitely looking up. A sense of hope and security entered our lives. A short lived one, however. Sadly, there was another glitch coming that would remain forever imprinted in my mind.

My parents had only been married a short time. I was playing outside in the sweltering heat that's part of living in the desert of Arizona, and I'd come in to get something from my room. My bedroom was located in the back of the house, directly across from my parent's room. As I marched down the hallway to turn left into my room, movement caught my eyes. Turning to look into my parent's room, I saw my dad, number four, with a woman who lived across the street from us.

I froze. In all honesty, there's a part of me that remains immobilized in that carpeted hallway even today.

I quickly spun myself around as if I'd just encountered a vicious animal, and now desperately needed to escape from its deadly claws. I took a few steps and quietly hid myself in the hallway bathroom next to my parents' bedroom door. I silently shut the door, leaving the light off, hoping the beast would go away. After what seemed like an eternity, I noticed two shadows at the bottom of the bathroom door. To this day I don't remember leaving, or how I got out of the bathroom. I don't remember eating dinner that night, speaking with anyone, or going to bed.

Walking through the mud of abandonment is painful, and leaves many questions. It's never easy when you watch someone walk out the front door of your home, and life, forever. Maybe just as difficult is having someone remain a part your life, but never give you the kind of love and support you hope for and deserve. They never walk out of your life, but they never truly walked *into* your life, either.

If there's a bright side in all of this, I learned a valuable lesson on forgiveness the next day. Apparently my dad had discovered that I'd been hiding in the bathroom. Perhaps he saw me sneak out. I can only conclude that he realized I saw everything and might tell my mom. Sometime between me escaping the bathroom and the following afternoon, he confessed his sin to my mom. That same day she approached me and asked me what I'd seen in the bedroom the day prior. I stood face to face with my mom, pretending it never happened.

How does a nine-year-old tell his mom that her new husband was in bed with another woman? Perhaps I had only dreamed or imagined it. I lied to protect her—and I suppose to protect myself. Eventually I divulged the entire incident, but only after she continued to press me for the truth. Without question, this was the most difficult thing I'd ever done in my short life.

She stood there and peered deep into my blue eyes. It was then that she reassured me that things would work out. My mom had forgiven him, and that was that. It was never mentioned again. My dad never said a word to me about what happened. No apology. No asking of forgiveness. No anything. It was as if it never took place. His silence only reinforced my own lack of trust toward men. How could I ever trust a man again? All men are liars, abusers, unfaithful, and connivers. I'd only seen men leave my life, my mom, and my family. And now I'd seen my dad with another woman—and then act as if it never happened. I don't ever remember seeing that neighbor woman again.

Understandably, it wasn't long before we packed up our things, sold our home, and moved to Phoenix. Perhaps the memory of that afternoon was too difficult for my mom. Perhaps she could no longer trust him. In the three years we lived in Phoenix we moved an additional *six times*. Looking back, it seems we were always searching for more than a house to live in. We were searching for *home*. After three years in Arizona, the military transferred my dad back to California, and three years after that we made our way to Nebraska.

Between the time I began kindergarten and my high school graduation I moved at least 18 times, and lived in four different states— moving to one state twice. These are just the moves I can recall; there may have been more. While these moves were due to new assignments for my military dads, many moves were also the result of running from past mistakes, flawed relationships, and emotional ties. I can't remember every school I attended, but I believe I entered at least 11 different schools during this same period. Each new school meant I was introduced as a "new student," because we transferred sometime during the school year. I can't begin to express how I resented being the new kid on campus.

"Class, let me have your attention," the teacher would say. "I want to introduce you to our new student, Rodney _____."

Fill in the blank with the last name of the dad I had at that moment.

Often my introduction was met with snickers or cold stares from the boys and girls in the class. Classmates were immediately judging me on my looks, clothes, how I stood, my facial expression, and how I walked. Whether this was true or not was inconsequential. This is how I imagined it each time.

The constant rejection I felt, real or imagined, as I stood at the front of the class served only to deepen my already pronounced insecurities. Over time I learned how to read people in order to fit in—but without getting too close to anyone.

Rejection is a cruel enemy. I've heard that rejection is the only emotion we feel that affects the same area of our brain as physical pain. In other words: rejection hurts!

Literally.

I began to anticipate rejection with each new person or situation.

I found myself walking into multiple settings with my guard up, believing it would be only a matter of time before someone wouldn't want me there. I interpreted the smallest movements of body language, lack of eye contact, the way someone said something (or didn't) as a sign of rejection. I became incredibly good at scrutinizing others, many times to a fault. Sometimes I would interpret things that may not have been accurate.

Rejection was my only friend.

This allowed me to make excuses for why I was the way I was. I had an excuse: I'd been hurt or wounded. This became my rationale for not attempting something. I could justify why I wasn't able to attend an event or finish a project, or why I wasn't able to give a task my all. I wanted to fail. As strange as it sounds, there was security in failure. The bankruptcy of my life showed others the tremendous emotional scars that plagued my life. There were simply too many wounds.

If someone did happen to pay me a compliment, I would quickly dismiss it.

They're just saying that because they feel sorry for me. If they only knew who I was or where I came from.

Externally I was dealing with new dads, homes, and schools. Internally I found myself battling my identity and self-worth. What did I do to cause my dad to leave? Why didn't the other dads stay? What was wrong with mom, my family, or me? Was I really only worth a five-dollar bill?

"So be strong and courageous! Do not be afraid and do not panic before them. For the Lord your God will personally go ahead of you. He will neither fail you nor abandon you" (Deuteronomy 31:6).

I was one card in a deck of 52, constantly shuffled, played by someone, or simply discarded, all to serve their own advancement and desires. Every new dad in my life served as a reminder I wasn't good enough for the last one. After all, I was the oldest. The other siblings had their dads and grandparents to go visit—or have their relatives come and visit them. I had no one. No dad ever visited. No grandparents called. I never received birthday cards or Christmas gifts from my dad or his parents. No one ever spoiled me. There was a reason new dads didn't stay long in our home. I could only conclude it had something to do with me.

Today I've come to realize that my dads' choice to run off wasn't my fault. But as a boy it was practically impossible to see that truth. God had work to do in my life, and desperately wanted to do that work, to bring restoration to my life. There would be paths on my journey I wouldn't like, detours I wouldn't understand, and U-turns that frustrated me. God would use each one to bring about healing. He does the same in your life.

I once read, "There are no easy roads to beautiful destinations."

God had something beautiful for me, but my journey would include some unpaved roads.

I didn't know this at the time, nor did I know the extent of the transformation I needed. My ability to correctly respond to life's struggles would play a huge role in my understanding of my value and purpose. My path to an abundant life would take me through some valleys, demand I learn to walk humbly, and require genuine tests of faith.

It was as if I was in that station wagon again. Though moving forward, I was looking backward. I've come to see that the Shepherd of my soul was moving me forward as I looked back. I couldn't see where I was going, only where I had been. This was His graceful healing in action.

Hearing that prophetic word while visiting Oakland, California, was part of the backward journey God was leading me on, since I was born in Oakland. God spoke of a stream bursting forth–the voice of the Lord and His love for me. Was it more than coincidence that it occurred where all of this began? I think not.

Rod at age 5 with his step-brother

CHAPTER THREE

THE ORANGE INCIDENT OF 1968

The enemy of your soul is far more frightened over who you'll become in the future than who you were in the past.

"Now all glory to God, who is able, through his mighty power at work within us, to accomplish infinitely more than we might ask or think"
(Ephesians 3:20).

My stepbrother was four, and I was a mature six, when we found ourselves living in a rented house surrounded by orange trees. Since we weren't trained in the formal art of harvesting oranges, and we were too young to harvest our own, oranges would plummet to the earth. This left the ground below cluttered with hundreds of disintegrating, round orange juice containers.

One sunny day we, being the good Samaritans that we were, decided to collect the damaged oranges and rid our small orchard of them. We agreed to toss them across the highway conveniently located at the end of the driveway. After collecting several rotted oranges, we headed to the highway and began throwing them across the busy road. We soon found that hitting the cars was much more fun.

Soon a car we didn't recognize maneuvered into our driveway. Being the oldest, and realizing that I was the man of the house, I had to do all I could to serve as guardian. Positioning myself between our home and the vehicle, I asked who they were and why they were heading to our house.

Out stepped an elderly woman to tell my brother and me that she was going to speak to our mom. Why is it that the little old ladies are always the ones who get young boys in trouble? Coming to grips with this age-old truth, we did what any young boy would do: We high-tailed it for the other end of the orange grove. We figured we could live off oranges. Vitamin C is good for you, right? We had plenty of shade and would never have to face the wrath to come.

One thing you must know. Most of the time, my mom was as nice as anyone you could ever meet. When we got in trouble, however, she was capable of punishing us to the point of a near-death experience. There was at least one beating where I believe I actually saw Jesus waving me in. After a few moments of hiding among the trees, I heard my mom call.

"Rodney Michael!" she yelled.

You know you're in trouble when one of your parents screams your middle name. We reluctantly made our way back, where we received the lashing of our lives—followed by bed without dinner. I'll never forget the orange grove incident of 1968.

Our punishments were quite harsh, to say the least. Perhaps it was the result of my own mom's abrasive upbringing. The fact of the matter is that many tend to act out in the same manner they were treated. It's only through genuine healing that we can change the trajectory of our lives.

If there's a story in the Bible that seems to illustrate how a life can be changed, it's in the fourth chapter of John. I must have read this story a hundred times, each time longing for the healing and change we see in the woman at the well to take place in my mom. Not for my sake alone, but for her sake. For those not familiar with the story, Jesus and the disciples were on their way back to Galilee, which took them through Samaria. Jews would typically travel *around* Samaria due to their disregard for Samaritans. Like a mom avoiding the candy aisle while shopping with her kids. Simply put: not someplace you'd want to be.

One thing I've learned in my quest with Jesus is that there's nothing left to chance. Jesus' path this day was not an accident. He chose to purposely travel through Samaria when He and the disciples come to the Samaritan village of Sychar.

Jesus sat waiting at the well while the disciples went into town to get some food. While He waits, a woman approaches the well to draw water. It's noon. Normally women would go in the cool of the day, certainly not at noon. Who wants to carry containers of water back to town in the heat? No one, but for some reason this woman travels alone to fill her containers.

Gathering water from the well was a time for the women of the community to get together, similar to how modern-day women go shopping, get their hair done, or have lunch together. It's tragic the lengths some go to in order to accommodate their pain. Often people would rather change the outward than go through the internal process of healing.

Upon arriving at the well, a conversation took place between Jesus and the woman. This one conversation is the longest discussion between Jesus and another person in all of Scripture, and it takes place with a Samaritan woman. This is significant for a couple of reasons. Women weren't to engage with men in conversation in private, and Jews and Samaritans didn't speak to one another—period. Jesus is clearly sending us a message.

It's not a coincidence that this one conversation takes up a chapter of Scripture. We see this seemingly tense moment played out later when the disciples return from town with food. They're shocked to see Jesus speaking with this woman. But this is much more than a chance meeting between two people. Jesus had been working backstage, designing this life-changing scene for the Samaritan woman. This one act would ultimately change the story for this woman, and bring value and purpose to her life.

We're told the woman had been married five times, and was now living with a man. And here she was in a dialogue with a single, Jewish man. What's truly amazing about the whole thing is that the dialogue brings a complete change of heart, and sweeping lifestyle transformation for her. You really have to read the story to grasp the intensity. After her encounter with the man she returns home to tell her entire village how a man changed her life. I'm sure people thought, "We've heard this before." How unfortunate that those closest to a situation are often the ones who have the hardest time believing.

A woman whose life was plagued by multiple rejections, by multiple men, finds renewed purpose. She went from being abandoned to living with abandon. I love this story because it shows how Jesus never gives up on us! He goes out of His way to ensure one woman never has to go to the well alone again. Out of His love for the woman, He shows her the power of forgiveness. As a result, she makes the decision to forgive those who've brought so much pain, disappointment, and abandonment to her life.

Her future is about to drastically change. Every person in her community knew her, and her lifestyle. She'd spent much of her life being neglected by men and women. But with Jesus' help, she determines to live in her purpose by putting her past behind her. It would have been much easier to go back home and pretend the chat with this Jewish man had never happened, or that it wouldn't make a difference. Instead she shares her life with the very people who turned their back on her. She repurposes her pain.

I think this story stands out so much to me because it reminds me of my own mom. Although my mom wasn't married as many times as the Samaritan woman, the similarities seem all too real. My mom spent much of her life in and out of volatile relationships. She endured unhealthy marriages, with unstable men, trying to find genuine love and happiness. It seems my mom made many a trip to the well, in the heat of the day, alone. Much of her life was defined by always searching for that elusive something or someone who would silence the demons of her past.

Not only did my mom spend much of her life alone, but she spent a great deal of her days running to escape loneliness. She would go to the well in search of life-giving water, only to have to search the next day, in another city.

Alone.

She wasn't just searching for a better well; she was trying to escape the abandonment she felt at the previous one. I guess this is the reason I read the story of the Samaritan woman differently than the other stories in the Bible. In both women I see someone who is desperately trying to love and be loved. I read about the Samaritan woman and I'm extremely curious about her background. What led her to multiple relationships, and then brought her to the place where she felt it necessary to travel alone? Did she have a family? Had they turned their back on her also?

How many times had she been utterly forsaken by someone she loved, or someone she thought loved her? How many times had she been abused, mistreated, or rejected by another, to the point where she thought it essential that she avoid all contact with other women in her village? How many times had she cried herself to sleep as she lay next to a man she had only just met?

How many times had she walked the dusty streets of her community, only to hear the faint whispers of others as they pointed fingers and turned away in complete disgust? How many times had she questioned the motives of another in order to protect herself? How many relationships had she manipulated so as not to get hurt? So many "how manys"!

It's even more difficult for people to escape their pasts today. The Internet, and social media, mean that our choices and mistakes are there for the world to see—and there forever.

It's baffling that others can so easily condemn someone without first taking time to listen to their story. I'm not condoning the sinful behavior of anyone—including my mom or me. I'm only suggesting that we listen to people's stories. It's difficult to hate, reject, or ignore someone once you hear his or her story. This is what Jesus did on that hot day.

He listened to her story.

When we think of Jesus, we think of a man who willingly placed Himself on a cross in order to take away the sin of the world. We think of someone who healed diseases, raised the dead, and cast out demons. Here Jesus wants us to know Him as someone who listens.

He listens to your story. He pays attention in order to offer hope. So much so that the woman no longer felt she needed to make the noon trip by herself. From here on out she would make the make the journey with the other women.

When we read through the life of Jesus, we see He had some incredible interactions with women. In Luke 7 we see Jesus raise the only son of a widow woman, and then in John 11 we see Jesus give Mary and Martha their brother, Lazarus. Mary Magdalene, Joanna, and Susanna not only followed Jesus in His ministry but also supported Him in His travels (Luke 8.1-3).

Mark 5 tells of the woman who had endured a blood disorder for 12 years, and who reached out and touched Jesus. A woman touching a man went against all social norms and acceptable behavior in the culture of that day. And someone with a blood disorder wasn't supposed to touch another person at all. But Jesus turns her act of "rebellion" into a moment of compassion, healing, and validation. He then calls her His daughter.

Jesus uses the example of a persistent widow in Luke 18 to model for us how to pray. In Luke 21 He shows us how to give generously by pointing out the poor widow who gave everything she had in the offering.

Again in John we find Jesus restoring a woman caught in the act of adultery (John 7.53-8.11). Prior to telling her to no longer sin, He tells her He doesn't condemn her. In other words, He speaks of her value first, and then deals with her sin.

This gives us some sense of how Jesus dealt with women. With each conversation, male or female, Jesus' attempt is to help us realize our value by first finding our identity in Him. Our sin doesn't define our value. Christ's death divulges our worth. It was the significance Jesus saw in us that led Him to a cross to eradicate our sin.

The Bible is full of women the Holy Spirit wants us to know about. For most people the first who comes to mind is Mary, the mother of Jesus. Let's not forget Elizabeth (Luke 1) and Anna (Luke 2). The book of Luke alone speaks of 24 moments in Jesus' ministry where He meets or refers to a woman, and each time He does so with healing, compassion, respect, and love. Acts 9:36 identifies Tabitha, also known as Dorcas, who's mentioned as a female disciple of Jesus, and who sacrificially supported other widows. Simply put, women were important to Jesus and He set out to bring value and purpose to all women. I wonder how different my mom's life would have turned out had she experienced such an encounter.

I mention this because, in the many conversations I've had with my mom about her relationship with Jesus, she continually responds with her own sense of guilt and shame for the life decisions she's made. She struggles to accept Jesus' love, forgiveness, and healing in her life. She struggles to allow Jesus to forgive her, to love her, and help her find worth. Finding mercy is too great an obstacle for her to overcome. For her, the hurdle of disgrace she feels from the many relationships and poor decisions is too high for her to jump.

Mom, the beauty of God's love and forgiveness is that He's jumped that hurdle for you. You don't have to jump.

He's jumped your hurdles as well!

Having empathy for another person is about having the capacity to understand a person's actions and feelings. It means doing more than simply listening to their story. It's about walking in their shoes long enough that you feel the impressions their feet have left upon the soles of their shoes. Each impression tells the stories of burdens that weigh on them. Listening to someone's story, and offering help, is a way for each of us to feel the weight of sorrow and pain residing in their soul.

I often think back to the violent past my mother went through, and the mistreatment she received by others. Of how she passed on the same to those she loved. This doesn't excuse her from the decisions, but it does help me to do my best to treat her the way Jesus treated others. To bring value to her.

In the last verse, in the last chapter, of the book of John, he writes that if all the things Jesus did were to be written down, all the books in the world could not contain the many things Jesus did. In other words, we can conclude that Jesus did many more miracles, and there are numerous stories and conversions that aren't recorded in Scripture. And I'm sure many of those discourses involved women.

But the stories we do read in the pages of the Bible are the ones the Holy Spirit chose for us to read, apply, and use to aid us in finding meaning. Each story presents us with the truth that the God of the universe cares deeply for each person.

I once heard someone say that God solved His first problem following creation by creating a woman.

"Then the Lord God said, "It is not good for the man to be alone. I will make a helper who is just right for him" (Genesis 2:18, emphasis mine).

A woman.

Up to this point everything God did was met with, "and it was good." Here we find it was not good. So God dealt with the problem by introducing woman. She was His solution to the loneliness God saw in the man He created.

I'm including this chapter because in some ways this chapter is a dedication to my mom and her efforts to be a good woman and mom in light of her sordid past. I genuinely feel sorry about the pain she experienced from constant abuse and abandonment. Unfortunately, this isn't just true of my mom, but so many other women. So this chapter is also dedicated to the many women who have gone through their own seasons of abandonment, pain, and heartache. May the faithful God gently speak His grace and restore joy, blessing, peace, and purpose to your life. Simply put: May He smile upon your life.

I mentioned that I struggled with trusting men in my life, but I don't have those same issues with women. If anything, I've always felt a tremendous respect for women, especially those who have experienced life's harshest blows. Now you can see why John 4 is such a meaningful one for me. It's my prayer that it will resonate with you. Putting myself in a woman's shoes is painful (I'm speaking metaphorically of course, but it would be quite painful to do so physically). But it has helped me in understanding my mom's sadness, and extending forgiveness to her.

I told you before that when I was 19 years old Ed told me the story of the five-dollar bet and how my mom and dad weren't married. Up to this point my mom had always told me that they were married. I imagine she did this to protect me, and to have some sense of dignity given her sordid past. For years I didn't say anything to my mom; I never wanted her to feel as though she wasn't loved because of a blind date on the beaches of California.

One day as we were driving I sensed the Holy Spirit nudge me to tell her I knew. I turned and said, "I know that you and dad weren't married. I want you to know that I forgive you and that I love you."

I didn't mention the five dollars. I'm not sure she even knew about the bet, and I wasn't going to be the one to tell her. I can only imagine how devastating it would be to discover a crude bet had resulted in her pregnancy. Tears began to cascade down her face. The weight and burden of carrying around another secret had been lifted from her, and she would no longer have to bear the load.

It's interesting how a few simple words can change the course of one's life. My mom and I now had nothing to hide. The darkest secret in her life was now in the light, where it lost its power. Perhaps this is one reason she confides in me more than any other person—along with the fact that I'm the only man who has remained faithful to her throughout her entire life.

Today I have the incredible privilege of traveling all over the world, speaking to teenagers and adults, many of whom are girls and women. During many of my sessions I'll kneel down on the stage in front of the crowd, and on behalf of those who have mistreated the young ladies of the group, ask them for forgiveness. Forgiveness for every time a father or husband has abandoned her. Forgiveness for every time a boy or man abused, deceived, took advantage, spoke ill of, or rejected them.

Each time I kneel I'm reminded of the pain a woman carries in her heart. Often someone, with tears in her eyes, will stop me to express their sincere thanks—with words or a hug, but always with deep emotion. I'm reminded of how different my own life would be if I chose not to forgive, but instead went through life angry at my own abandonment. It's so easy to point the finger of blame, but holding onto your past keeps you in your past.

So to all those reading this at this moment, on behalf of all those who have brought you sorrow through abandonment, neglect, abuse, or rejection, I ask you to forgive. I'm not asking you to live out the remainder of your life as if it didn't happen; I'm only asking you to live the remainder of your life without the burden of carrying your jar to the well.

Alone.

Please forgive.

Please allow yourself to be forgiven.

Please allow yourself to be loved again.

What I find so fascinating about the Samaritan woman was her determination to put what she just experienced into motion. Immediately she went back to her community to share all Jesus had done in her life. The day she had a talk with Jesus was a turning point for her and her future. No longer did she need to question her value or identity. She had found it in a man who brought her life. That same Jesus does the same for you and me today. He brings life and healing in the midst of our past.

God in all His wonder reversed this story in order for me to find living water. My only youth pastor was a woman. I look back on this and see the hand of God in it. I didn't trust men. Would I have surrendered my life to Jesus if I'd heard about Him from a male? I'll never have to answer that question. So it was that in 1978, when female youth leaders were extremely rare, I found myself hearing more about Jesus. Much like the woman at the well, my life has never been the same.

Following Jesus meant that I, just as the Samaritan woman, would have to learn how to love and forgive. A huge aspect of the healing Jesus wished to do in my life had to do with forgiving rather than blaming. Loving rather than remaining bitter. Embracing faith rather than living in fear. John 4 had to become real for me so that I could show a real Jesus to my mom. She had to see Jesus was able to bring her life-giving water. The same water He'd brought to me.

Your life has eternal purposes. There's a God who has His hand on your life, regardless of the shame and disgrace that has bombarded you. It's my hope that you have an encounter with the Christ who loves you and forgives you. May such a meeting forever change the trajectory of your life. May you no longer have to travel alone.

Rod at age 3

CHAPTER FOUR

BISCUITS AND GRAVY

The tough times you are going through offer eternal purposes.

The phone rang one afternoon while I was spending a weekend at the home of Ed and Margaret in Nebraska—the couple who introduced my mom and dad. I would often stay with them on the weekends while attending college in Lincoln, as this would allow me to attend church. My family was living in England due to a military transfer, and I'd decided to attend school in the States rather than make the journey across the pond.

The decision as to stay in the States or go to England was a genuine struggle for me. Deep down I knew I had to remain in the States for my own sanity and spiritual growth, but I did love my family and felt a certain level of guilt in remaining behind. My mom was especially critical of this decision. After all, I was the only one in her life who had remained with her, and now I'd be leaving.

There are times when we all need to establish boundaries in our lives—restrictions in place simply for survival. This was the case for me. I determined it was best for me to remain, as my home had grown more and more unhealthy. As I grew older I saw and heard more of the abnormal behavior that surrounded our home. I knew to travel with my family would cost me spiritually, and I could no longer afford to remain in this environment. This may sound cruel to some, but the day-to-day toxicity had reached its peak for me. I needed to break away.

Sadly, as one grows up in a dysfunctional home, most of the memories seem to be negative, and tend to negatively impact lives. Despite growing up in a volatile home, there were a few good memories, but they don't seem to carry the same punch or occur as frequently as the unhealthy ones.

Life was an emotional roller coaster. One moment we could be sitting on the couch as a family, laughing at a sitcom. Moments later we were being greeted with irrational yelling, extreme manipulation, and one-way guilt trips. Moods changed faster than one of us could change the channel, leaving us dumbfounded as to why the sudden outburst. The only thing more difficult than an emotional explosion was an unexpected surge of accusations for something you didn't do. Sometimes it was just easier to admit to something, even if you didn't do it.

There remained an unhealthy fear in each of us whenever one of our parents walked through the door. I learned early on to guard every word and each action so as to not create a more precarious situation. I would carefully contemplate every possible response in order to offer the one answer that would bring the least amount of fury. To this day, my wife and children accuse me of taking too much time to reply to the most basic question.

Living in our home was like being blindfolded while walking on a high wire, and without a safety net. There was no one to guide you, and each forward movement had the potential to lead to disaster. So I learned to judiciously guard each word, every action, and all facial expressions, hoping to not upset anyone. I sometimes wonder if my responses today are the genuine me or remnants from my past.

What I hadn't anticipated was that my decision to stay would open the door for the Holy Spirit to create intense healing moments in my life.

I was handed the phone and told it was my mom calling from England. This was before cell phones, so a call all the way from England meant something quite significant. My mind immediately put up the security fence I'd grown so accustomed to building. In just a few seconds I had run through all the possible reasons for a call. It wasn't a holiday or birthday. Perhaps I had overlooked something. This left me unnerved. Fear set in.

I stood in the kitchen waiting for my mom to speak.

"Are you sitting down?" my mom asked. "I have some bad news."

A million thoughts raced through my mind.

"What is it?" I cautiously inquired.

"Steven's been murdered."

He was my mom's first husband, and my second dad. My stepbrother's dad. I only remember seeing him a couple of times in my whole life, but he was once my dad. What I do remember about Steven was his medium build, fair complexion, and short blonde hair. How did my mom want me to react? She had asked me to sit down. Was this her way of telling me I should feel sadness? How did my mom feel about this news? After all, she was once married to him. Was this just information she was passing along? What feelings should I have? Then it occurred to me to ask a safe question.

"How was he killed?" I asked.

This was more than a safe question. It was the right one to ask. I didn't have to express feelings with this question. Choosing facts over feelings was a sure-fire way to avoid saying the wrong thing. To be honest, I wasn't sure I had feelings. I've discovered over the years that abandonment often leaves one without many feelings. Any emotions that are there are often negative and self-damaging, so I avoided them as a way to cope.

My mom went on to tell me he was a police officer working undercover, covertly working himself into a narcotics gang. Someone in the mob exposed him and had a hit put out on him. One morning he went to start his car, and it suddenly burst into flames from the blast of a bomb. He'd been assassinated.

I'd become pretty good at reading my mom over the years. She would confide in me, often placing her trust in me rather than her husband. I could sense, over the thousands of miles, that the news of her previous husband's murder had left a huge hole in her heart. Though they'd been divorced for some time, one of her husbands was now gone—and in a horrific manner. It was a subtle reminder that another part of her life had died, too. Someone else had left her.

Abandoned kids often grow up way too fast. Being the oldest meant I was thrust into the role of counselor, healer, and trusted friend. Unfair. Especially when I'm trying to figure things out on my end. There were several times when my mom would pull me aside or call me long distance just because she needed a man to speak with in whom she could confide. My mom had shared many a secret with me over the years. This also meant that I felt all the more awkward around the men who entered my world. I was told things about them that they didn't realize I knew. If my mom struggled to trust them, why wouldn't I? Why hold any hope that such a father-son relationship could ever exist? These men weren't my dads as much as they were my mom's husbands.

The first man I do actually remember as my dad was Dan. I must have been about six years old. During this period of my life I recall four significant memories that shaped my way of thinking about family, people, God, and me. The first occurred while we lived in New Mexico.

In our family, living paycheck to paycheck was the way of life. There were several times when my mom would come to me and ask to borrow money from my piggy bank just so we could eat, or have money for gas or her cigarettes. Over the years I acquired odd jobs and saved money, partly because of what occurred in our own home when it came to the handling of finances. I had determined at an early age that I never wanted to live this way.

Needless to say we didn't have much by way of clothing, gifts, outings, vacations, or special meals. We always had a roof over our heads and food in our stomachs, and for that I remain extremely grateful. I say all of this to lead up to my first memory. On several Saturday mornings we would make a trip to Dan's parents, my step-grandparents, who also lived in the same town in New Mexico.

These mornings were especially memorable because my grandma would make us homemade biscuits and gravy. To this day I love the smell and flavor of biscuits, smothered in a thick layer of gooey happiness. I remember as a young boy, standing on my toes, peering over the stove to catch a glimpse as grandma stirred the creamy, white delight in the black cast iron skillet. This was more than breakfast. It was a reminder that I was part of a real family. A tradition that captured my heart.

We had a dad and mom. We had a grandpa and grandma. We would go to their house and have biscuits and gravy. If I could plan out my last day on earth, my A.M. meal would consist of this glorious meal. This sporadic morning ceremony gave me hope that we were as normal as the family down the street, and that better days were ahead. Each bite brought me closer to this reality. This custom was short-lived, however, which leads me to the second noteworthy memory.

Dan had been in the Navy but this was no longer the case. I was too young to understand all the reasons why he couldn't seem to hold a job. I do remember he always had a new form of employment, newfound energy, and new dreams of becoming a rich man. He continually sought after wealth. This attitude toward money meant Dan always had vast ambitions to bring in more wealth. This led to moving from town to town in search of greater opportunities. Money was one of his gods.

So one day Dan pulled up in the driveway of our home in a large truck, filled with several bags of red apples. He was now in the roadside apple-selling business. You don't see this as much today due to farmer's markets and large grocery stores, but growing up in the 1960s, this was fairly commonplace.

"Do you want to sell some apples with me, Rod?" he asked me one day. "You can ride in the truck and miss some school. We'll have some fun and make lots of money. We'll be partners."

I remember sitting shotgun in this old black truck, filled to the top with apples. I was in business with dad. I felt important. We would park on the side of busy highways, put out our signs, and wait for people to stop by for our delicious fruit. Once again, hopes of normalcy would slowly make their way into my life. These hopes would soon give way to deeper wounds and further abandonment.

This was the first time I recall doing anything of this magnitude with a dad. It wasn't fishing or hunting. It wasn't a sporting event or car show. It was, however, a father/son outing of sorts. My intention isn't to take anything away from my mom and the sacrifices she made, but this was dad and son. Every young boy needs this relationship in his life. It helps solidify a young boy's identity.

Our roadside business outing was short-lived, however. We had parked our truck, and he asked me to watch it so he could cross the street to "take care of some business." As a young boy I didn't know what this meant, but I really had no choice. He trusted me and that was all that mattered at that moment. Looking back I realize he was crossing the street so he could have a few drinks, and perhaps boast to others about his business. This was his way of dealing with the harsh realities of life.

As he was sharing his disappointments in life, a nice, elderly couple pulled up next to our truck and made their way over to me. I was the apple salesman and would be handling the family business while my dad was away. I recall it as if it were yesterday. What I didn't remember was how much a bag of Red Delicious apples cost.

"Did you make any sales while I was gone?" Dan asked.

"Yes sir," I replied, feeling somewhat proud of myself.

My pride was cut short, however, as he asked me how much I had made while he was gone. It was only then that I discovered I had undercharged the couple and actually lost money on the sale.

In just one moment I saw how upset my dad could be become. I don't know if it was from the alcohol, or because we desperately needed every cent of income, or if he just thought I was incapable of ever measuring up. Perhaps all three. All I knew is that I had failed. A part of me died that day. I felt as undervalued as the bag of apples that had passed through my hands. How dreadful that an innocent mistake, even at a young age, can leave such a huge scar.

Over the next several months I noticed my dad acting very differently. Apparently his alcohol intake increased to the point that he would come home drunk—bringing periods of rage and abuse. None of the mistreatment was directed toward my siblings or me, but toward my mom. There were times when I would walk through the door to see my mom on the floor, straddled by my dad, as he repeatedly hit her. My mom would tell me to go outside or to the neighbor's until he was done. This is the third memory of my third dad.

I wasn't big or strong enough to do anything about it. I had no choice but to turn and walk out the door, waiting for an all-clear sign. Terror was constantly with us. It was the anxiety of another dad leaving—or worse, one remaining who would hit my mom or one of us.

What made this even more difficult was there were periods when Dan was extremely nice. Times when we would laugh and play catch, or he would take us on a family outing. As wonderful as these times were, however, they were often momentary and only brought about confusion once the cruel times returned.

Dan and my mom weren't married for long before it was apparent to them that this match wasn't made in heaven. Once again, divorce rocked our home. One day he was no longer there. Maybe this was God's protection over my life. Maybe it was because I was only a child. Maybe I chose not to remember. Maybe I just didn't care.

A few years later we found ourselves living in Phoenix, Arizona, with my mom now married for the third time to my fourth dad. I was getting ready to play a soccer game when Dan showed up at our home with his new wife to ask his two daughters, my stepbrother, and me if we wanted to get a treat. I was asked to sit in the middle of the front seat and was immediately shown five thousand dollars in cash, sitting in his new wife's purse. This was his way of showing me he had made it in life. I had never seen him more proud.

At halftime of the soccer game my mom gathered my teammates and said, "Guys, I want you to yell out 'Whitlock' as loud as you can during the second half. I want Rod's other dad to hear his name is Whitlock now."

I stood next to my friends completely humiliated. How dare she ask my friends to get involved in our families' dysfunction?

The second half is a complete blur to me. Funny how a young boy can vividly remember a two-sentence conversation at halftime but not any portion of the second half of his soccer game with his friends. Did I score a goal? Did we win? I have no idea.

I was mortified that my mom would pull my teammates into this. What was even more upsetting was my name really wasn't Whitlock. Sure, that's what my friends at school knew me by, but legally my name was something different.

There were several instances where I remember being embarrassed by what my mom would say to my friends. As a parent, I realize this is a part of life for every child. I'm sure I've embarrassed my children a few times (sometimes on purpose), but it was different for me. I felt my friends and I were always being drawn into some elaborate grown-up game we didn't understand or want to be a part of. There were no rules in this game, or if there were no one explained them to us. A part of me cringed each time she spoke to someone, anyone, but especially my buddies. I know I shouldn't have felt this way, but I did.

This would not be the street I would have chosen.

My first dad had abandoned me.

My second dad had been assassinated.

My third dad was an alcoholic and extremely abusive.

My fourth dad? That's another story.

July 29, 1973

DEAR MOM,

HOW ARE THINGS. THINGS ARE FINE
I LOVE AND MISS YOU VERY. HOW ARE GIRLS
AND BA-BA. HAVE YOU BEEN GOING SWIMMING.

THE FOOD IS GOOD HERE. IS ~~THE~~
THE WEATHER THE SAME DOWN HERE
THE WEATHER IS COOL DOWN HERE.
THERE ARE ABOUT 150 BOYS HERE.
I'M IN CABIN #12 AND JEFF IS
IN CABIN #14 WE PLAY FOOTBALL,
SOFTBALL, VOLLYBALL, AND PING, PONG.

I SURE HOPE EVERYTHINGS O.K.
WHEN ARE YOU GOING SEND SOME MONEY?

WELL GOODBY I'LL RIGHT LATER.

Love

ROD

CHAPTER FIVE

THIS IS MY SONG!

People are more concerned about deleting their Internet history than they are in making history.

"Do not be afraid or discouraged, for the Lord will personally go ahead of you. He will be with you; he will neither fail you nor abandon you"
(Deuteronomy 31:8).

We snap a picture on our phone. Immediately we eyeball it, carefully examining every detail of the image. Delete. Take another, from a different angle. Apply a filter. Then we meticulously edit. Approve. Post. Check back every so often to see how many Likes, comments or heart-shaped emoji's we received. Repeat.

There are no do-overs in life. No edits. No deletes. No new angles. We're stuck with the snapshot that was taken.

Such was the case for me while living in Phoenix, Arizona. Mandatory choir was a part of the fifth-grade curriculum. Every day my class would join our voices together in perfect harmony. All right, that's a slight exaggeration. Like most fifth-grade boys, I made my way to choir because I had to, not because I wanted to sing my lungs out. I wouldn't have chosen choir. My first love was sports. I played just about every sport that was offered. Choir wasn't a sport, so I had no interest.

I can recall several specific plays, scores, victories, and games, but other than one particular day I don't remember anything about choir. It stands as one of the most humiliating days in my entire life. It also serves as a snapshot of how I felt many days growing up—a photo forever framed in my mind. How I would have loved to hit Delete and ask for a re-take.

I was standing on the front row, directly in front of the piano and our choir teacher. I don't remember his name but I do remember his checkered suit jacket; bushy mustache; thick, round glasses; and larger-than-life head of curly hair. Standing on the front row had its advantages. No one would be able to hear me sing. No one, that is, except the choir teacher.

"Something doesn't sound right," he said, as he stopped playing the piano and scoured the class. "I want everyone to hold this note," he said as he hit the piano key. Don't ask me which note it was. Give me a B and I can flatten it!

While the entire class sang that note, our frizzy-haired teacher slowly made his way down the line of students, turning his ear toward us as he passed by. I stopped singing as he approached. He paused and asked me to sing. I did. I mean…technically I sang a note. Just not the one he asked for. At this point I received an invitation to move to the front of the class. Usually this meant someone was going to sing a solo. This was not the case for me.

"Go stand over by piano," he said to me.

I walked over to the ivories, my entire class watching me. Our choir teacher hit the upright again and asked the class to belt out the note. I was asked not to sing this time.

"Oh, that sounds so nice!" Mr. Plaid Jacket said. It was humiliating.

Ever feel like life is holding a big party and you're not invited? Ever felt like everyone else is singing the same song, and you can't sing—or perhaps you're asked not to? Not only are there no re-takes, you're not even allowed in the picture. For you, the only time you're in the photo is if you photo-bomb it.

This wasn't the first time I was singled out for my lack of ability.

My sophomore year of high school I played football, and I was terrible. I may have been a better singer. I was third string, only because there wasn't a fourth string. Our varsity team had lost their first game and, as you can imagine, the coaches were livid. The head varsity coach shouted that anyone not giving 110 percent during each and every practice would be told to go stand by the equipment shed. This would serve as a way to completely humiliate you in front of your peers.

Apparently I missed a block; I was immediately scolded and told to run to the equipment shed. I was the only player to be sent to the shed the entire year—I was also the only one ever told to stand by the piano.

People can be cruel. Perhaps you've wondered why someone you cared for or loved would abandon you. Why you were left standing alone. Why you were mistreated. Why you were neglected. Why you experienced the pain of rejection. You play scenes in slow motion, focusing on each frame, trying to catch something, anything, you missed the last 100 times you replayed this.

Hurting people hurt people.

The more we ache, the more we end up wounding others. Social gatherings become nightmarish. We wander into a group of people immediately looking for an escape. Each gathering becomes a painful reminder of the rejection we've felt a million times and serves to remind us that no one really wants us in his or her photo. No one wants us to sing. Our emotions become elevated to mountainous proportions. We feel lost in a sea of nameless faces. We want to sit by ourselves in a room and let life pass by.

Even when someone welcomes us to their little cluster we tell ourselves that they're only doing it out of pity. Nevertheless, we join—convincing ourselves this group is different from all the others. They really want us to sing with them. You find yourself growing paranoid until you reach your personal boiling point. You notice others no longer listening. Apparently you're not singing good enough. You quietly excuse yourself from the group. You spend your life anticipating rejection from others. You search for it at every gathering and, sadly, you seem to find it.

Jesus understands.

He knows what it's like to sing with others and then be asked to no longer sing.

"Then they sang a hymn and went out to the Mount of Olives" *(Matthew 26:30).*

After eating a meal with His disciples, and washing their feet, Jesus sang in a choir with His closest friends. He's moments away from the Cross, where He'll be separated from the choir. People will mock His lyrics of comfort and healing. Jesus understands what it's like to feel the pain of being abandoned.

To stand alone.

"At noon, darkness fell across the whole land until three o'clock. At about three o'clock, Jesus called out with a loud voice, 'Eli, El, lema sabachthani?' which means 'My God, my God, why have you abandoned me?' " (Matthew 27:45-46).

Jesus cries out in a loud voice, asking the same question you and I have asked. Surely His own Father would stick by Him. Surely He wouldn't be forsaken in His hour of greatest need. But Jesus calls out to His Father, asking the question, "Why did you abandon me?" He experiences the heartache of His Father's displeasure at man's sin. Jesus was now, for the first time, grasping the full impact of being separated from His Father.

Jesus wasn't just alone; He was completely surrounded by darkness. The Light of the world found Himself surrounded by unexpected blackness. Never in all of history has anyone faced a darker period than those three hours. Jesus is in a battle for the souls of people. Your soul and mine. Family and friends. Co-workers and people we've never met. He's in pitch-black darkness in order to bring light.

The one crucial instant in history when Jesus most needed His Father, God stepped out of the photo. Jesus experienced what each of us experience when we engross ourselves in sin. Jesus' whole purpose for coming to the earth had come to fruition. He came not simply to be a good teacher or bring temporary help to others. He came to give His life as a ransom. He came to take our place. He descended so we could reach up to the Father, to spend eternity with Him.

The irony.

Jesus separated from the Father so we could be joined in eternal relationship with the Father. Jesus went through the feelings of abandonment so we would spend eternity never having to know the anguish of isolation. Jesus, the Light of the world, immersed in nightfall so we could live in the light of God's presence.

The first time I experienced my own feeling of separation from God was during this same fifth-grade year. My brother and I were playing football in our front yard on a Sunday morning—since church wasn't a part of our weekly schedule. I threw the ball to my brother when a palm tree intercepted my pass. We spent the next several minutes trying to retrieve the ball from the palm tree with no luck. It was then that a van parked itself in front of our house.

A man stepped out of the church van and asked us if we wanted to go to Sunday school. We told him he would have to ask our mom, but first we asked if he could rescue our football from the palm tree. Little did I realize that, just as the tree had intercepted our ball, Jesus was in the process of intercepting me. So the following Sunday my brother and I retired our jerseys and found ourselves in the van heading to the Baptist church.

For several months we sat through both Sunday school and the adult service. I say sat through the adult service, but in reality it was more like sleeping through. Each Sunday we would delay our entry into the service so as to spend the least amount of time there. Sunday school was filled with snacks, games, and prizes, but the Sunday service sounded like adults speaking on a Charlie Brown television special.

Because we delayed going into big church, we often ended up sitting on the front row, since the back pews were taken by early birds. I was a veteran when it came to playing football with my brother, but I was clearly a rookie when it came to securing a back-row pew on Sunday morning. I still wonder if our falling asleep on the front row in any way affected the pastor's confidence in his preaching. Perhaps a few therapy sessions helped.

My initial journey as a Christian was short-lived but I do recall two significant events. The first was finding myself standing in a McDonalds, calculating how much it would cost to get a hamburger, fries, and a soda. The man who faithfully drove the church van had secured permission to take my brother and me out to talk about Jesus. I must admit I was far more interested in the lunch destination than the eternal destination of my soul.

Seldom did we eat out as a family, and going to McDonalds was a rare privilege. Remember, this was back in the 1900s.

The three of us sat in a booth, enjoying our meal, when the man who drove our van began sharing what it meant to receive Jesus into our hearts. I don't remember how this happened or what I needed to do, but I do recall him talking about the beast in the 13th chapter of Revelation! The mood at our booth quickly changed from enjoying our meal to being alarmed that one day I may become a Happy Meal for the beast. Why an adult would preach this particular message to 10- and 8-year-olds continues to baffle me.

My second recollection regarding my introduction to Christianity came a few months later. My mom was asked if the church could sponsor my brother and me to attend church camp. My mother had no problem saying yes, since it would mean a week with two fewer kids in the house. So off we went to an all-boys camp in July of 1973. I would spend the week in cabin 12—my brother in cabin 10.

During one of the evening services an invitation was extended to receive Christ as our personal Savior. I was still unfamiliar with this language and how to respond. My church know-how consisted of falling asleep during services. I sat there with a conversation going on in my mind. One voice urged me to walk forward to the front—to put feet to my decision to follow Christ. A second voice worked to silence the first voice. I listened to the second voice. But the entire time I felt something in my heart, compelling me toward a relationship with Jesus.

Following the service, and some recreational time, we returned to our cabins to bed down for the night. I pulled my camp counselor aside and replayed the struggle I had just gone through during the service. I told him I wanted to surrender my life to Jesus. So, sitting on the bottom bunk of cabin 12, I prayed, surrendering my life to Jesus.

A few days later the speaker invited all the boys who wanted to dedicate their lives to serving God to come forward. This time I eagerly stepped out from my seat and made my way to the front. I wasn't going to miss another invitation.

Following a prayer at the altar, the speaker asked those who had responded to follow him outside to meet. We sat at a picnic table and for the next several moments he proceeded to tell us what it meant to dedicate your life to serving Jesus.

I have no way to confirm it, but I believe that every boy who responded that sunny day in July is in some way serving Jesus today. That moment left such an indelible mark on me that I still recall where I sat on that bench. The speaker was at the head of the picnic table and I was sitting on the end, just left of him. Little did I realize how prophetic that decision would be in my life.

Upon returning home, my brother and I discovered that our family had moved. Don't worry…we were able to find them! This move put us out of the reach of the Baptist church van, so we'd no longer be able to attend Sunday school or church. Much to the relief and self-esteem of the pastor, I suppose. No church meant Sunday morning football games were back on the schedule, with the benefit that our new home was absent of palm trees. This would be the last time I would hear about Jesus for five years.

I was reintroduced to Jesus between my sophomore and junior year of high school, while living in Nebraska. My best friend, Rich, invited me to attend his church youth retreat. Several of his invitations were met with an emphatic no from me, but he continued to ask. Getting me to attend his youth retreat proved to be more difficult than getting me on the Baptist church bus. His determination paid off and I finally agreed to attend. It was on this retreat, in July of 1978, that I recommitted my life to Jesus.

So many emotions flooded my life that night as I realized God's hand had been on me over the past five years. The bottom bunk of cabin 12, the altar in the camp chapel, and the end seat of the picnic table appeared to me as some sort of deja vu. These grace-filled, gentle reminders from God served to let me know that God had not forsaken me as so many others had in my past. God once again extended to me an invitation to me to be part of His plan and purpose. He made room for me in the photo. He invited me to sing.

What makes this part of the story so improbable is that I wasn't even supposed to be in Nebraska during my high school years! My father's next military assignment had come through prior to the completion of my eighth-grade year, while we were living in California. We were to be transferred to the island of Okinawa over the summer following eighth grade, and I would most likely graduate from the military school on the tiny island in the Pacific. We had our passports, and had received all of the necessary vaccinations in order to make the voyage. It was literally at the last moment that my dad's orders were altered. We would be moving to Nebraska rather than the Pacific.

I sincerely believe God has a specific purpose for our lives, and often brings it about with a sense of humor. Rather than move to an island, we would find ourselves moving to the middle of the United States, about as far from an island as one can get. Our move would mean the sunny skies, warm temperatures, and sandy beaches of island life would be substituted with wind, sub-zero winter temperatures, and roadways covered with salt thanks to winter snow. We'd received several shots in each arm for our vaccinations, but this extreme change of scenery was a whole different shot in the arm.

Looking back, I can't help but believe God was orchestrating my life down to the finest of details. Though I'm not sure why we'd been scheduled for a transfer to Okinawa, only to find ourselves in Nebraska, I'm sure God had a plan and purpose behind it. Some may call these moments nothing more than a coincidence, but I prefer a term I heard from someone once: a Godincidence.

We go through life asking God to adjust our circumstances for our own comfort, but He adjusts our journey for His purposes. One of those purposes is to transform our lives. Though it may sound nonsensical to assume that God would have the U.S. government change an entire families' military orders in order to see me receive Christ, I can't help but wonder what my life would be like if we had moved to Okinawa.

Would I have ever had the chance to renew my relationship with Jesus? Would I have been in ministry? Would I have met my wife, Kim? Would I have ever had the opportunity to use a snow shovel? I don't know the answer to these questions, although I can assume life would be drastically different for me.

I often consider the following verse of Scripture in thinking back upon this time in my life. *"From one man he created all the nations throughout the whole earth. He decided beforehand when they should rise and fall, and he determined their boundaries. His purpose was for the nations to seek after God and perhaps feel their way toward him and find him—though he is not far from any one of us" (Acts 17:26-27).*

God intentionally purposed in His grand scheme of things to dictate the time of my birth and the places I should live. I have to believe this if I'm to believe that I'm more than an accident, a mistake, or the result of a five-dollar bet. God determined ahead of time that this particular time was the perfect moment in all of history for me to find Him.

In other words, I could have been born 1,000 years earlier, or 20 minutes from now, but God chose the timing of my birth. I could have been born in Denmark or South Africa. This seemingly inconsequential detail was anything but that. These events not only gave me the best chance to find Him, but confirms that He was thinking about me long before my birth! I was on His mind before the creation of the world (Ephesians 1:4). You might say I've always been on His mind. The good news is that this holds completely true for you, too!

God's plan and purpose for my life was wrapped up in me moving to Nebraska. There I renewed my relationship with God, was baptized, was called to ministry, and married my amazing wife and began a family. This was simply a continuation of my journey with God. What I thought was an error by the government, or inconvenience, turned out to be a God-led detour.

In reflecting back on my life, I came to a realization. It was July when that five-dollar bet took place. It was July when I spent four nights in cabin 12, and found myself dedicating myself to serving God. It was July when I attended a student retreat, rededicating my life to Jesus. I believe, in some way, God was speaking a message to me. That bet seemed to be a July mistake, but it turned out to be a July miracle.

"But to all who believed him and accepted him, he gave the right to become children of God" (John 1:12).

I was no longer a child with no value, no future, and no hope. I'd become a child of God, the Father.

Others may have turned their back on me, but God never did. Fathers may have left me, but my heavenly Father has not. And He hasn't abandoned you. I sincerely believe that, at this very moment, while you read this book, your Father is speaking to you. Reminding you of how He orchestrated events in order to gain your trust. His supreme desire is to increase your belief, that He might bring healing and freedom to your life. It's my hope that you allow Him in your photo. It is my sincere hope that you will enjoy singing with Him.

The blind hymn writer Fanny Crosby penned these words.

This is my story, this is my song,

Praising my Savior, all the day long;

This is my story, this is my song,

Praising my Savior, all the day long.

Despite going through life blind, Fanny chose to sing! The last line of this song, "Blessed Assurance," ends with, "Filled with His goodness, lost in His love." I think another way to saying it would be, "abandoned in His love."

"For the Lord your God is living among you. He is a mighty savior. He will take delight in you with gladness. With his love, he will calm all your fears. He will rejoice over you with joyful songs" (Zephaniah 3:17).

Can you hear Him?

God is singing over you!

Songs of deliverance. Songs of comfort. Songs of healing.

The best part? He sees you standing next to the piano, alone, and invites you to sing with Him.

CHAPTER SIX

FINISHING SECOND

"Stop making what people did to you bigger than what Jesus did for you." –
Christine Caine

*"Don't be afraid, for I am with you. Don't be discouraged, for I am your God.
I will strengthen you and help you. I will hold you up with my victorious
right hand"* (Isaiah 41:10).

There were two men who had a profound impact on my life, and both
happened to be coaches. Over the summer of 1970 I moved from Paradise
Valley, Arizona, to Phoenix. Once again, I found myself being introduced
as the new student. Mr. Edwards would be my gym teacher for the next
two-and-a-half years, before we moved back to California.

I loved his class. I guess it stems from my love for sports. Athletics
were a way for me to escape from my life at home, both physically and
emotionally. In addition to providing me a diversion, I found that sports
allowed me an opportunity to show others and myself that I had value.
Mr. Edwards challenged me, encouraged me, and treated me like I
belonged to a family.

Gym class in the '70s was a whole lot more challenging than it is
today. Every day the entire class would run a mile before engaging in
activities. Yep. I ran a mile every day, in the Phoenix sun, September
through May. Good thing it was a dry heat! I became pretty good at
running. By age 10 I was able to run a mile in about six minutes.

Every day of class I would finish second in our mile run just behind my friend, Bryan. He always finished first, and between fourth and sixth grade this would be the order of finish. I never beat him. Ever.

Mr. Edwards was also a staunch believer in registering our school in many citywide athletic events. We participated in football, cross-country, soccer, basketball, track—just about every sport you can think of. There were actually Saturdays when I found myself involved in two sporting events on the same day. I would run cross-country in the morning followed by a soccer game that afternoon.

During one particular cross-country meet I rounded a few trees on the course and saw Bryan a few yards ahead. I had never been this close to him. Either I was having a particularly great run or he was having a bad one. We were nearing the finish line when I remember thinking, *I can beat Bryan!*

There's an interesting story found in the Bible of a woman who was desperately searching for love. You might say she was in a race also. Not a race against another, but a race against herself. It's the story of a woman named Leah. She was the eldest of two daughters, neither of whom was married. Apparently Leah had grown up in a well-to-do home, but with a dad who was bent toward manipulation and deceit. Leah's dad's name was Laban. Perhaps you've heard the story. Either way, let's take a quick peek.

Laban was approached by a young man name Jacob who enthusiastically wanted to marry Leah's younger sister, Rachel. Rachel was beautiful. Jacob wanted to marry Rachel so badly that he agreed to work for Laban for seven years in order to marry her! That's commitment, or love truly is blind.

For the next seven years the entire family and their neighbors would hear about the agreed-upon wedding between Jacob and Rachel. Everyone heard, including Rachel's older sister, Leah. Jacob pulled out his iPad and set the countdown timer, indicating when the seven years would be up. It's sad that more people never experience this kind of devotion or love from someone.

Rachel was beautiful. Leah…not so much. No one seemed to want Leah. Laban probably thought that in the seven years Jacob was working for him, someone would agree to marry his older daughter Leah. You see, in Laban's culture the older daughter had to marry before you could give any of the other daughters. The four of them began praying for Leah to get hitched, none harder than Jacob.

But after seven long years Leah remained single. Unwanted. Seven years of listening to Rachel telling her older sister of wedding plans, the house they would live in, the make and model of the camels they would own, and the names they would give their children. Seven years of watching a young man, day after day, tirelessly work himself to exhaustion for her younger sister. With no one coming to the door to see if Leah was available for a double-date with Jacob and Rachel. Constantly being reminded she was not good enough for another.

Laban must have been a crafty man, because after the initial seven years, Laban convinces Jacob to work another seven years for his daughter. Rachel must have been extremely beautiful and pleasant for Jacob to agree to such a demand. Jacob was obviously head over heels in love. Leah was devastated. Each day that went by served as a reminder to Leah that she was the reason her sister and future brother-in-law weren't married. *Surely Leah will find a husband in the next seven years,* everyone must have thought.

Regrettably, some stories don't end up happily ever after. Seven more years passed and Leah was still single. Laban had run out of time, but not ideas. This is where manipulation and deceit insert themselves in the story. I've seen these two enemies destroy relationships and families time and time again.

You were whispered sweet promises of love only to find those whispers turned into shouts of anger and abuse.

You were told you were the only one he loved, only to read a text he sent to another.

She promised you the world, only to have it come crashing down on you.

You were told it would be forever.

You were promised it would never happen again.

You were abandoned…again.

It was now Rachel's wedding day. She had endured a 14-year engagement. That's crazy! We're now just hours away from the big moment, when Rachel's dad Laban enters the bridal chamber. He clears the room of family and friends so that only he and Rachel remain. Laban then conveys his diabolical plan of deceit to his youngest daughter. Leah is to walk down the aisle and marry Jacob.

Rachel shouts, "What? I will not do that, dad!"

"Shhhh, we have guests. I need you to do this. Leah has to be married and this is her only hope," he says. "I've run out of ideas. You'll still get married to the love of your life, just let me do this first."

The conversation would continue for some time. Harsh words would be exchanged. Many tears would be shed. But being the good daughter and sister she was, she conceals herself for the remainder of the day. She doesn't even attend her own wedding. Her dad had already picked the hiding spot for her. He had been planning this for months.

Laban now approaches Leah. It's her turn to hear the sinister plan that's about to take place—one that includes her as the main character. She reluctantly agrees, perhaps to honor her father. Or perhaps out of love for her sister. Or maybe she believes this in the only way she'll ever be able to marry. She thought about how Rachel walked, carried herself, and motioned with her hands. Leah would have to sell each guest on the idea that she was Rachel, including Jacob.

Leah, now veiled to conceal her true identity, would be the bride. Abandonment aims to conceal your identity. It wasn't the way she'd envisioned her wedding day, but perhaps she'd given up on the thought of ever having her own ceremony. She was part of a sham. Jacob would be deceived. Guests would be betrayed. How long before the truth of the lie would come out?

It wasn't long before social media buzzed with the scandal.

Of course, that night Jacob discovered the truth. It wasn't his intended next to him, but her sister! I can only imagine the thoughts running through his mind as they lay there. Why? Where was Rachel? Was she part of this? Laban! I worked 14 years for Rachel and ended up with Leah. I wouldn't work 14 minutes for her! What just happened? Where's the hidden camera, because this has to be a prank!

Rachel had been set aside. Leah had been abandoned. Jacob had been misled. Abandonment leaves behind a trail of wounded people. Rumors must have been flying throughout the community. Reputations were tarnished. Feelings were hurt. Close friends were left in shock. Lies grew bolder. All of this from one simple act in the name of love, and one solemn search for a genuine relationship.

Reminds me of the beginnings of my own story in 1961.

Once the dust had settled from the day's activities, another wedding was held. This time the wedding would be for the right couple, Jacob and Rachel. It must have been awkward, to say the least. How many friends showed up? After all, they'd been lied to once... The maid of honor was now the matron of honor, who was married to the groom, who would become the husband of the sister-in-law! The groom would be the brother-in-law to his wife, who was the matron...oh, never mind.

Leah must have been shattered emotionally. The Bible goes so far as to say that she was hated by her sister! She did what came naturally to her, knowing that she wasn't good enough to get married on her own. She questioned her worth. She would devise her own ruse. After all, she had a good teacher in her father. He had created many a deceptive plan in his life, and Leah had taken good notes. Her plan was to give Jacob sons so he would love her more than Rachel.

Growing up with a mom who had seen her own share of abandonment gave me a bird's-eye view of how deceit manifests. Deceit is the first cousin of abandonment. It works its way into the lives of those who've found themselves forsaken, rejected, and discarded. Just like Leah, I learned how to navigate the murky waters of deceit and manipulation.

On more than one occasion I found myself subtly manipulating a family member or friend. I would manipulate a conversation to secure my own position, or to ensure the outcome would have greater benefit for me. Most times I wasn't even aware I was doing it. It had become a part of my character. It wasn't until years later that I realized just how disturbing my behavior had become. I can only attribute my dark behavior to my need to protect myself from further hurt, rejection, or once again being abandoned by another. I'd become extremely good at this awful behavior. It only goes to show how far the pain had travelled throughout my life.

One of the most valuable lessons I've learned through my experiences in life is that the more I attempt to be in control, the more I lose control. If I truly surrender my life to Jesus and His plan, then I must completely relinquish all. This includes my emotions, my thoughts, my attitudes, and my will. God wants to set me free! Free from sin. Free from the pain of abandonment. Free enough to once again see my potential value.

Back to our story: Recall that Leah wants to give to Jacob a son so he will find worth in the wife he didn't choose on his own. Leah delivers her first son, and names him Reuben. The names Leah chooses for her children are very important and we should examine each one. Names tell us a story, and we get a glimpse into her thoughts.

In the Hebrew language, Reuben means, "See, a son." Certainly Jacob would love Leah now. She was able to do what Rachel could not, as Rachel was barren. This was Leah's way of shouting to Jacob, "See, I've given you a son!" But as barren as Rachel was, Jacob's love for Leah was just as barren. Apparently one son would not be enough to turn the heart of Jacob toward Leah. Once again Leah was left questioning her own value.

Again, Leah delivers a baby and names her second son Simeon. Simeon in the Hebrew sounds like the word for "heard." In other words, she was proclaiming that the Lord had heard her cry to be noticed and loved by her husband. Surely this son would change things in the house of Jacob.

Silence.

Levi was the name of her third son and it sounds like "attached." *Now my husband will attach himself to me for giving him three sons,* Leah must have thought. Three sons, and Rachel hasn't given him one. Yet a third son had little to no effect on Jacob. He continued to love Rachel, even though he was also married to Leah. Meanwhile Rachel remained childless.

There are times when we attempt to earn the love of God or others by doing enough "good things," only to be deeply bruised when we realize nothing we do can earn us His love. The abandonment Leah felt in her life from the two men she held most dear was too much. Her dad seemed to have no faith in her. Her husband had no love for her. How could she continue to live life attempting to please others who seemed to care little for her? She was without hope.

This was my plight the day I turned the corner to see Bryan running just ahead of me. For just a second I felt I could beat him, only to have every fiber of my being scream out, "No you can't; you never beat him. You won't beat him today or any day." I was destined to finish second. Again.

There's nothing wrong with finishing second. I know some of you have a t-shirt or bumper sticker that reads, "Second place is the first loser." The truth is that second place is pretty good. The tragedy is that I never believed I was good enough to finish first. Being the result of a five-dollar bet, and having multiple dads leave me behind, left me stumbling through life believing second was as good as I could ever be. Slowly, over time, I began to believe the lies that my value to God and others was, at best, a second-place finish—the first loser. Yes, God still loved me and others liked me but it was only because they were under obligation to do so. This is what I thought.

So it was that one day God captured me with this truth of Scripture found in Genesis 29:35. Leah had her fourth son. The culture of her day would have suggested that she was a rock star wife. Sons were a sign of God's blessing. Leah having four sons was so much more than simply being one shy of a basketball team. It was the name she gave to her fourth son that stood out to me this particular day.

She named her fourth son Judah, which sounds like the word "praise." I believe it was on this day that Leah came to a place in her life when she determined that she would praise God in the midst of her second-place finish. She would do her best to give God all her praise—in the good times and in the dark ones. It was a turning point in her life.

What I find even more fascinating, however, is that the author of Genesis tells us that Leah stopped having children. Here's how verse 35 reads.

"Once again Leah became pregnant and gave birth to another son. She named him Judah, for she said, "Now I will praise the Lord!" And then she stopped having children" (Genesis 29:35).

Did you catch it?

The writer tells us she had no more children! The problem with this statement is that she *did* have more children. As a matter of fact, after giving birth to Judah, Leah would have two more sons and a daughter. Why would the writer state she was finished having children, if she would clearly have more children?

This story is laden with back-stories, underlying motives, and rich truths from Scripture. Leah had come to a point in her life when she realized that trying to earn meaningful love on her own would prove futile. Leah had to come to realize that only in her praise to a loving Father would she understand how to love and be loved.

It wasn't that she had to muster up enough praise to God in order for Him to love her. Remember, there is nothing we can do in and of ourselves to earn God's love. She came to grasp that though life can be completely unfair, that life mistreats us, that sometimes we are dealt a bad hand, we can choose to live in a place of complete contentment. We can choose to live in a place of total satisfaction that moves us to a place of life-long peace. It's from this place of laying our lives down that we learn to worship, even when our lives are filled with chaos.

Praise positions us for His presence in our lives. It's in our praise that God reveals Himself to us and for us. It's in these moments that God unveils more of His plan for our lives.

Perhaps you are reading this and feel as if your entire life has been made up of manipulation, deceit, and lies. You've experienced the pain from being discarded or the heartache of rejection. You're reading in search of answers to the hurt you've carried for far too long. There's hope that is found in surrendering your life to Jesus, that instant when I put aside my own attempts to earn enough of God and acknowledge that it is well with my soul. You, God...are enough.

My second-place finish served as a picture of God's grace in my life. I can't help but believe one reason that memory stands out so much is not to discourage me into thinking that I'm not a winner, but rather to encourage me to run hard in order to bring courage to others to run harder. In other words…don't give up! Ever. Keep running, even if there's no chance you'll finish first.

Perhaps there have been moments in your life that you believe you were wrongfully deceived or manipulated. Perhaps there have been times when you gave it your all and it didn't seem to be good enough. Can I challenge you to have the audacity, the grit, to continue running in a world that often throws in the towel? And what happens when you can no longer run? This leads me to the second coach who made a huge impact in my life.

Physical injuries had taken their toll on my body by the time I reached my junior year of high school. As a result, I was told to avoid running, and my doctor suggested I try swimming. This would serve as therapy for my legs. My mom then suggested I try out for the swim team as a way to get the therapy I needed and remain active in competition. So I started swimming in November of my junior year of high school.

It was my first day of swim practice that I discovered just how bad a swimmer I was. My coach, Mr. Green, had little faith in me, since not only was I the slowest on the team but I had never swum competitively. So it was that I was relegated to the slow lane with a couple of other swimmers. Over the course of the year I greatly improved my times, as I continued to swim during the off-season. By the start of my senior swim season, I had shaved a considerable amount of time off the previous year and was now one of the fastest on the team.

During the first week of practice the team was asked to vote for the captain. Everyone wrote down their choice and handed the papers to our coach. The team then proceeded to head for the locker room. Moments later Coach Green made his way to the locker room, walked over to me, and extended his hand to congratulate me. I had been chosen captain. It was that day that I saw on my coaches' face what I had longed to see on just one of my dad's faces. To this day I can see Mr. Green's face, indicating how proud he was of my hard work. My determination had paid off.

I had finished first.

So I say to each of you: Keep running, even if you aren't the fastest. Your running helps others gain confidence in their own race. I have to believe that my challenging Bryan that day made him a better runner. Keep swimming, even if you're the worst on the team. Your grit may inspire others to jump in the pool.

CHAPTER SEVEN

NIGHTMARE AT THE DRIVE-IN

"Adopting one child won't change the world; but for that one child, the world will change." – Unknown

During eighth grade I had a best friend named Jim. He was in ninth grade but had to repeat a grade, leaving him 16 as a freshman. This was awesome for me as this meant my best friend had his license. Jim also had an older sister, probably 18 at the time, who had a boyfriend of 20.

It was the summer of 1976. Jim asked if I wanted to go to the drive-in movies with him, his sister and her boyfriend, and a few girls. Apparently Jim's sister had fixed him up with a girl she knew. This girl then talked a couple of her girlfriends into joining in. So we all piled into their station wagon with Jim driving and his date in the front next to him. Jim's sister and boyfriend were in the back of the station wagon, so it was me and two girls sitting in the middle row. The movie that night was "The Texas Chainsaw Massacre." Not a movie a 14-year-old should be seeing, but remember, I didn't grow up in a home with convictions. So a show like this was certainly within my boundaries.

Halfway through the flick, the girl seated next to me, whom I had never met before, placed her right hand on my left thigh. Remember, I was 14 and she was 16. Also remember, we were watching a horror movie, and it was coming to the peak of the scary part. I was terrified. Not just from the picture and its gore and butchery, but the fact that this older woman had strategically placed her hand on me!

You see, no one had ever talked to me about proper relationships with a girl before. The father/son Sex Talk wasn't just a neglected conversation; it was a foreign concept. I'm not sure if this talk never happened due to a dad not being around long enough, or a dad not feeling "dad" enough to approach the topic with someone else's son. Regardless of the reasons, I sat there in a terrified state. Not necessarily from the movie, although it was scary enough, but from a much older woman using me as a handrail.

I became more and more tense as the chainsaw roared—and as her hand progressed. In a moment of utter desperation I yelled out, rather loudly, "I'm so nervous!"

Of course, everyone in the car thought I was just an immature 14-year-old not able to handle a petrifying movie, when in fact it was a shout for help. Even after proclaiming my panic, her hand remained glued to me, much like that of the creature gripping his chainsaw. It wasn't until the end of the movie when we were driving off that her hand and my leg parted ways. I think the indentation from her hand remained for a week!

Looking back on that night of horror (leg, not movie), I'm reminded how important it is for a son to have a dad-to-son talk to about relationships, dating, marriage, and sex. Throughout my teen years I recall a couple of instances when I longed to talk to my dad about such issues but always felt extremely clumsy.

"Such love has no fear, because perfect love expels all fear. If we are afraid, it is for fear of punishment, and this shows that we have not fully experienced his perfect love" (1 John 4:18).

Fear was a huge part of my life. Whether it was a girl placing her hand on me, or the events to follow, I lived in fear, without His perfect love.

In September of 1976, we moved from the small military community of Atwater, California, to Nebraska. This move occurred a few weeks into the start of my ninth-grade year. My fourth dad had been transferred to the Strategic Air Command at Offutt Air Force Base in Bellevue, Nebraska. Once again I began the school year a few weeks after everyone else. This, of course, meant that I would be brought to the front of the room and introduced as the new kid.

"Class," the teacher would say, "I want to introduce you to our new student, Rod Whitlock."

She may as well have said, "I want to introduce you to Rod Whitlock, an incredibly uncomfortable, insecure, embarrassed, self-conscious, incompetent student."

I can't begin to tell you how uncomfortable this was for me. You'd think it would get easier since I was a gold medalist at new-student introductions. What's amazing about this whole process is that, unbeknownst to me, God was using this experience in my life as part of His overall plan—one that wouldn't reveal itself for several years.

I've always been a bit shy and quiet by nature. Perhaps this was a result of growing up the way I did. With most moves, and there were several, I was brought to the front of the class to be introduced. What made this move particularly difficult was the fact that the school year had not only already started, but I was entering school as a ninth-grader in a school that was made up of seventh- through ninth-graders.

This meant that most of the students in the school had grown up in the same elementary school, or at the very least had known each other since seventh or eighth grade. They had their friends and their routines, and didn't seem the least bit interested in adding any new ones. I found this especially true on the bus ride to school, and while hunting for a seat during lunch.

The morning trip to school was particularly degrading. Each day I would either be ignored or unwelcomed. The ride was an emotional roller coaster, consisting of a painful reminder that I wasn't free from the enemy of abandonment.

No one ever spoke with me. No one looked at me. I didn't exist. My bus stop was the final one before arriving at school, meaning that by the time I boarded the bus the entire front three quarters of the bus was full, three students to a seat, leaving the rear of the bus as my only option.

The back of the bus was made up of all the popular kids. One might term them the bullies of my generation. No one dared sit in the back, even if they had first crack at it. The final five rows of seats were off-limits. They were the only seats on the bus with two to a seat by the time the bus rolled to my stop. Every day of school during my ninth-grade year I walked the plank before getting thrown to the sharks. The decision of where I would eventually sit brought immense teasing for the students occupying the seat I chose. Ninth-grade boys can be extremely vulgar in the things they say. Never was a junior-high boy so glad to finally arrive at school.

Moving from class to class without any friends to speak with was a welcome relief following the inhospitable ride on the bus. At least I didn't have to listen to those around me use derogatory names because I had chosen to sit by them. Do the math. This meant that for approximately an hour and a half each week I would be brutally reminded of my worthlessness.

During the school day I enjoyed the freedom of finding a seat away from others and quietly doing my work. That is, until the lunch bell rang out. Finding a seat at lunch proved to be even more challenging than boarding the bus. At least with the bus I knew students had to let me sit down, since the bus couldn't move until everyone was seated. Discovering a place at lunch proved to be a different sort of test. The table I sat in yesterday was now filled with a new group of students, making it necessary to walk throughout the cafeteria looking for an empty table.

There were days when my search would take half the lunch period. At times I would cautiously approach a chair, only to discover that all the chairs had been saved. I soon learned this was not the case, however; the students just didn't want me to sit close. I quickly ascertained that I had to eliminate any table with students already engaged in conversation from my list of potential spots. I find it interesting how we adapt to the surroundings around us, even at the expense of our identity.

So I'd look for empty tables or tables with a few other unwelcomed students sitting down and silently eating their lunch. The fact that they were quietly eating meant they too were loners. Of course, we were all too insecure to form our own lunch table and establish a spot each day. Journeying through life, constantly feeling rejection, leads to assuming you're always going to feel rejected—too neglected to do anything about it.

It was during my lunch period in ninth grade that I ran into two other individuals who had spent much of their lives living alone. As a result our being labeled we found ourselves hanging out during the final moments of lunch. I wouldn't call us friends, for we never saw each other outside the few minutes we were together at the end of the lunch. We were more like survivalists. Following lunch, students had to wait outside for their next class. The three of us would often stand next to the building so as to not draw attention to ourselves. We spent the remainder of the period making small talk with each other until the bell rang. This welcome sound gave us permission to navigate the hallways to our next class and signaled the halfway point of our day.

The following year the three of us found ourselves at different high schools. Dan and Kyle went to East High and I went to West. Years later, I heard that a girl I'd gone to West High School with was brutally murdered. Her killer was one of the two guys I'd hung out with during lunch.

I can only conclude that he was unable to find a lunchroom table with friends during high school. I pictured him sitting alone and having no one to talk with. I'm not trying to excuse him; I just want to convey how difficult it is to go through life feeling abandoned. I look back on those days wishing somehow I could have made a difference in his life. How

I wish I'd been secure enough to help him. The problem was that I was attempting to find my own sense of belonging.

Perhaps this is the reason I've been serving in student ministry for the past 30+ years. It goes without saying that this is the reason God has called me to help students sort through their lives. I've been the captain for my high school swim team, was elected to positions of leadership by my classmates, made the National Honor Society, and made all-star teams in sports. I was also made fun of, laughed at, and went through seasons without a friend to sit with at lunch or even someone to say a simple hello to. My school life was a mirror of my home life, and those lives catapulted me into my purpose.

To add to my already unsettling life we moved five times during my freshman year of high school. At one point I recall my dad telling me we may have to live out of our car for a period of time, as we were unable to find affordable housing. I told him I would run away if that happened. There was no way I was going to live my life in a parked car. Of course, I hadn't considered the alternative. My life was chaotic enough. I'm sure that my attitude added to the stress my dad was already feeling in his life. As a 14-year-old boy I was unable to mentally deal with the reality of the six of us living out of a car while attending school. It's one thing to fit the six of us in a '70 Vette in order to run errands, but quite another to have a family of six sleeping in a '72 Impala. As it turned out, we were able to find housing in a trailer park. Later that same year my mom approached me, asking a question that would forever change my life.

"Rod, I have something I want to talk to you about," she said. "Here, sit down on the bed for a moment."

My mom proceeded to tell me that my dad wanted to adopt me, my stepbrother, and my two stepsisters. My dad had already determined he was going to do this but my mom felt it was necessary to ask me about it prior to it actually happening.

As the oldest, she *wanted* to know if I wanted to be adopted, and she wanted to let me know that the judge may ask me some questions about my desire to be adopted. This was quite a bit for a 14-year-old to grasp, but everything inside of me screamed out, "Yes!" After 14 years of living with no real identity, there was someone who wanted me. I would finally have someone who longed to be my father and give me his name.

I don't remember what I said to my mom that day, but my emotions were blaring with heightened excitement. To think that a father wanted to adopt me, a thin, dirty-blonde-haired kid with a single eyebrow, was vastly different from what I encountered throughout my previous years. Maybe now I could talk to my stepdad as a real dad, and share things with him—talk about life and girl stuff. When you think about those nasty bus rides and dreadful lunchroom moments, you can understand why my adoption was an easy decision for me.

From the day I was abandoned by my dad, to the time I was adopted, was 14 years. The same length of time Jacob had to work in order to be married to Rachel. Jacob waited and hoped. I waited, and hope found me. Maybe this is one reason why that story has left such an impression in my life.

No longer would I be a slave to my past and the confusion of who my dad was. Although he wasn't my biological dad, he wanted me. He adopted me. Family isn't as much about DNA as it is about acceptance and love. The last name that my friends knew me by would be the same last name that would be on my birth certificate, and in my school records. It would also be the one my wife would take, and my kids would be known by. I had received sonship. I would be adopted. There's something about going through life without proper identity. It leads to all sorts of puzzling thoughts and emotions.

Who am I?

The day of adoption finally arrived, with my parents, siblings, and me standing before the judge. I had already determined that I was going to tell the judge that my dad adopting me would be the greatest thing that has ever happened in my life. As a matter of fact, I was hoping the judge *would* ask if I wanted to be adopted. He was going to get an earful. This was going to be my chance to unload a weight that had been wrongfully placed on my shoulders.

We stood before the judge, lined up oldest to youngest. Here was my chance. I had formed my first sentence and replayed it over and over again. Ready. Set. And then it was over. Not one question. The judge didn't even look at me, much less ask my opinion on the matter. The whole process took just a few moments and we were now Whitlocks. I left somewhat disappointed. Not at what had just happened, but at *how* it had happened. I finally had something I could believe in…or should I say someone.

Within moments we were home, and that was the end of it. No celebration. No congratulations. No cake or ice cream. Our last name had changed, but that was the extent of change. Somehow I had it in my mind that everything was going to be different now. Certainly a change in last name would bring a change in our home life. At the very least I thought I would feel different. Now there would be more laughing, family outings, hugging, and security. Right? What I soon learned was that a simple change of last name brought me no closer to the utopia I had dreamed of.

It wasn't until a few years later I came across this verse in Romans. It was my reading of this verse that pointed me in the direction of hope. It stood out on that day and continues to today because of what happened when I was a 14-year-old boy.

"For you did not receive the spirit of slavery to fall back into fear, but you have received the Spirit of adoption as sons, by whom we cry, 'Abba! Father!' The Spirit himself bears witness with our spirit that we are children of God, and if children, then heirs—heirs of God and fellow heirs with Christ,

provided we suffer with him in order that we may also be glorified with him"
(Romans 8:15-17).

The God of the universe chose to adopt me and anyone else who calls upon Him. We can cry, "Abba Father" or "Daddy God!" God wants to be known by us and He wants us to know Him as a Father. The fantastic part of this is that I did nothing to earn this or deserve this. God, the Father, showered me with His outrageous grace and adopted me into His family. With this relationship we become heirs and have access to all He has for us. Why? Because He changes our name, giving us identity, and restores our future. We take on His name and He becomes our Father.

What's the big difference between this adoption and the one I experienced in ninth grade? Unlike the lack of celebration following my adoption here on earth, Luke 15:7 announces that all heaven rejoices, throws a party, and celebrates when one chooses to be adopted by God the Father. My last name had changed and I become a son. When you or I surrender our lives to God, angels sing out and dance around the throne of God. Music is loudly played across the heavens. A party breaks out!

A few years later, just prior to my junior year, my best friend in high school, and eventual best man in my wedding, invited me to a church retreat with his youth group. It was during this retreat that I rededicated my life to Jesus. This encounter came five years following the decision to trust Jesus while living in Arizona.

In May of 1980 my mom asked me what gift I wanted for my high-school graduation. A study Bible was my immediate response. My desire was to learn more about the Jesus I was committed to. Just a year later I found myself a small group leader for a bunch of energized junior-high students. Looking back I see how God took an insecure kid, who struggled through most of his school experiences, to a place of redemption. Not just for me but for the next generation of students. God was clearly directing my initial steps as a son. My natural adoption didn't change much more than my last name. My spiritual adoption changed my life, future, hopes, and dreams, and impacted the lives of those I would later meet.

The acceptance of a loving Father has allowed me to have the opportunity to travel all over the world and stand before adults and teenagers to share my two adoption stories: I wanted to be adopted by my earthly father, and my heavenly Father wanted to adopt me.

Remember that I was always the new kid being introduced to the class, and that God would later use it as part of His purpose. Over the past several years, as I travel to speak with teens, I'm always being introduced to a room full of people I don't know. God brought redemption from the pain I felt, and turned it around for His glory. He took the abandonment I felt and turned it into opportunities to speak to students about living a life of abandonment for God.

The moments I spent hunting for a lunch table in ninth grade serve as a reminder that there are students who are lonely in a crowded room. So during meals at a youth event I make it a point to walk past every table to speak with students, particularly the ones sitting by themselves. One day we'll be invited to a giant lunch table for what the Bible calls the Marriage Supper of the Lamb. You can read about this in Revelation chapter 19. The wonderful part about the Supper is that no one will have to worry about finding a seat.

All are welcome!

CHAPTER EIGHT

HAPPY SAILING!

Your ability to grow is tied directly to your determination to change.

Ed, the man who made the five-dollar bet with my dad, was as round as he was tall, with thinning, short brown hair. His smile was as large as he was and he exhibited a gregarious persona in every way. On the day he unveiled my birth circumstances, he remarked how my dad walked with a slight limp. This seemed to be a curious detail to mention. I look back and believe this attention to detail was his way of helping me come to terms with my existence. After all, in many ways, Ed was responsible for me being here.

"Your dad made a five-dollar bet that he could have sex with your mom that night. I took the bet, thinking it would never happen. By the way, your dad walks with a slight limp."

I'm reminded of another man who walked with a limp. His name was Jacob and his story is found in the first book of the Bible, Genesis. He walked with a wobble after wrestling with God. I'd say he's fortunate to get out of that wrestling match with only a slight shuffle! I know how Jacob received his defined walk. I'll never understand the circumstances around how, when, or why my dad developed his.

I believe God used Ed that day in a prophetic manner to convey a life-altering message to me. Why else would this one single detail be mentioned? Yes, Ed was unloading a burden he had carried around for several years, but he was also sharing a message, even if I didn't realize it at the time. I wasn't told my dad's hair or eye color, or how many siblings he had, or what his parents, my grandparents, were like. We didn't discuss how my dad decided to enter the military, or the job he performed. No mention of where he was from or how Ed had met him. He walked with a noticeable limp was the extent of information that was passed on to me.

There are moments in our lives when looking backward is a way for us to begin limping forward. For by doing so we end up seeing messages that help define our potential and our ultimate purpose in life. Your past is meant to serve as a trigger to propel you into your future.

I have to believe God wanted me to see more of myself in the pages of Scripture. Looking back I now see how God used that single piece of information so I could learn how to remain at peace in the midst of life's storms. Hearing that my dad walked with a limp made the story of Jacob leap from the pages of the Bible. It was as if God was saying, "You will also walk with a limp." Only my limp wouldn't be a physical one but a God-transforming hitch. You notice when someone has a limp. Their walk is a distinguishing feature. We mustn't forget that walking with God means we will wrestle with Him. I've done my share! Each match leaves us with a more pronounced hobble. It's as if God was using parts of my past in order to direct my future steps.

One of the great things about being a kid living in Phoenix is that there are several sunny days. This, of course, means lots of swimming. That is, if you can swim. I was in fifth grade and still didn't know how to swim.

One beautiful day my friends invited me to go swimming. I agreed. I'd been left out of too many things in life. It wasn't until we approached the pool that I realized that this swimming thing was about to get real. I would have to tell them I couldn't so much as doggie paddle. What I hadn't counted on was that confessing my lack of skills would be met with my friend's emphatic unbelief. I did my best to convince them that I couldn't swim right up until they threw me into the deep end of the pool!

I now know what it's like to be drowning.

Fighting my way to the top of the water, I desperately grabbed a breath, only to slide downward again. With arms flapping like a newborn eaglet, and slipping below the surface of the water for the second time, I once again made my way to grab more oxygen, just above the water line. I was heading down for the third time when I felt a stable hand grab my arm and pull me upward.

A dad who had been reclining while his children played in the pool saved my life. My friends stood stunned. It was on that day that I determined to learn how to swim. Desperation had changed my desire for change.

It's amazing how many people wait to change only when they're forced to. They receive a doctor report that unless they exercise and change their diet, they'll face certain disease or death. I constantly hear stories from people who avoid change out of fear. It's only when they're forced to change that some even bother attempting to do so. Sadly, many live their lives doubting God could ever do anything to turn their situation around. They go through life living defeated and unwilling. Sometimes we have to be pushed in the deep end before we realize it's time to learn to swim. As long as we go through life living in defeat, we miss out on the victory God wants to bring to us.

There are times when our past can actually hurl us to victory! The key is learning how to repurpose our past. Our purpose is found in discovering the power and potential from our past. God doesn't just want to heal our past, He wants to redeem it. Allow me to use the following illustration.

As I stare out the front windshield of my car, I do so through a large glass. Located in the middle, and toward the top, of this large piece of glass is a small mirror. One tool to look forward, and the other to view what's behind. There's a reason the windshield is larger than the mirror:

What's in front matters much more than what lies behind. But that doesn't make what's come before unimportant. Many people are afraid to look back at the memories and scars from the past, as they're too painful. We're afraid to admit we almost drowned…emotionally. What we must clearly see is that gazing into the mirror reminds us of how far we've come. If we exam it long enough, we find clues to what lies ahead. So I invite you to glance in the mirror for a moment. Not to relive the pain from the past but to clearly see how God walked with you and ordained the potential in your life.

Early in my Christian walk I embarked on one of those read-the-Bible-in-a-year journeys. Accomplishing this goal would both challenge me spiritually and, hopefully, increase my love for God and people. My journey carried me through Genesis, Exodus, Leviticus, and Numbers. Then I found myself arriving at the Old Testament book of Deuteronomy. I'd cruised through 22 chapters when I was dropped onto the wrestling mat, leaving me with a limp.

"If a person is illegitimate by birth, neither he nor his descendants for ten generations may be admitted to the assembly of the Lord" (Deuteronomy 23:2).

I stopped reading. My mind was racing as I set my Bible on the table in front of me. *Who put this verse in my Bible? God? Why would He do this?* Perhaps if I claimed I didn't understand the verse and simply kept reading, I'd be excused from it or it would vanish. After all, it was in the Old Testament. We live in New Testament days. Does a verse written several thousands of years ago still carry weight in my life? The Holy Spirit has a way of latching onto us through God's Word in order to communicate His heart to us. He takes our life experiences and uses God's Word to bring healing and direction for our lives.

I was wrestling with the Holy Spirit. He was teaching me something about myself, yes, but also teaching me something about Him. I was new in my faith with Christ and didn't understand how culture, customs, and context all played into understanding what was behind verses of Scripture. Questions began to plague me about whether or not I would ever be able to enter the sanctuary, welcomed and accepted by God. Was God now abandoning me?

I think many of us read our Bibles thinking God is looking for ways to painfully judge us or to show us how terrible we are. As though God spends His days trying to think up ways to make our lives miserable, or heap immeasurable amounts of guilt in our lives. Trust from God's Word can quickly be distorted, depending on what filter we use when we read it. It seems over time God's Word becomes more defined by the filters of our past. This greatly affects our view of God and His plan for our lives.

One thing I resolved in my mind that morning was that I would certainly be able to enter the sanctuary. After all, Jesus gave us access to God through His death on a cross and resurrection from the grave. At the same time, any hope of me ever being in ministry or serving as a minister of the gospel in the Church would be out of the question. My illegitimate birth would seem to automatically disqualify me from preaching from a pulpit, praying for the sick or new believer at an altar, serving communion, baptizing people, or engaging in other duties.

My journey to fix that bad filter, and draw a healthy conclusion regarding this verse, was a long one. Too many times we want the quick, easy answer to our questions. Our walk often includes days of struggles and contending for faith in Christ. This is meant to strengthen our faith, not defeat it. Don't mistake wrestling with God as Him being angry with you. With each match, my walk with God became more pronounced. I continued to place myself within the pages of Scripture. I had to wrestle with the reality of who God is rather than try to fit God within the pages of my own life. My filter needed to be dismantled.

God's grace overshadowed my life the more I wrestled. Just as Jacob cried out in his own match, I shouted, "Lord bless me!" I wanted to be blessed in order to be a blessing. This requires bouts on the mat. This allowed me the opportunity to experience more of His outrageous grace, leading me to a greater understanding of who I was wrestling. What I didn't realize at that moment was there would be more struggling and that God was taking me on a journey in order to solidify my calling and purpose for Him.

Years later this grace manifested itself in my life as I found myself on pastoral staff of a church in Nebraska. It was the same church where I'd recommitted my life to Jesus in July of 1978. Each day during the week the pastors would gather in the sanctuary from 8 to 9 AM for prayer. It was one of my favorite times of the day.

This was a time for us to connect with God prior to starting our day. It allowed me to speak with God and for God to share His heart with me. The pastors spent time praying for the needs of people, the community, and the church. One particular day God addressed something in my life that helped me put to rest Deuteronomy 23. My walk with God would forever be different.

I believe He continues to work His will in our lives with divine purpose and intent. He dutifully progresses through this detailed list in order to bring healing in our lives—a healing that leads to change. He wants to address our fears and insecurities, anxiety and sin, shame and doubts, and the areas of our lives where we feel defeated or discouraged. He wants to bring health to our soul. He also knows the speed at which we can handle such conversations. He knows what to say, when to say it, and how to voice it. He also knows where to say it, as you'll see in a moment.

Those of us who have children may understand this a bit more. As a parent, it's important that we choose the when, how, where, and what to speak with each of our children. Because they're unique, we approach them in a way that reflects our understanding of this fact. I've tried to do this with mine. I have to admit that many times I've talked with one of my kids in a manner that suggested anything but this. Fortunately we have a heavenly Father who gets us. He knows how we tick and approaches us with the gentleness and kindness we need so that we can receive from Him.

This was the case one morning in my time of prayer. I'd entered the sanctuary for prayer like any other day. It sat 2,500 people so it was large enough for each pastor to have his own particular place to walk and talk with Jesus. Mine was located under the balcony where I had an entire aisle to myself, from the back entrance of the sanctuary to the front. I would spend most of the hour walking along the wall, talking with and listening to God. It was our place, and He met me as an affectionate and deeply caring Father

So one day, as I was praying, God seized my attention and began to speak to me. He's always speaking to us, but on this day I heard Him whisper. He captured my heart. These conversations are meant to enrich our lives in order to make an impact on those we come in contact with. It was one of those instances I will never forget.

"I want to change your name," was the voice I heard from heaven.

I knew it was God for two reasons. First, this was something I'd seen God do in Scripture. On several occasions God had changed someone's name. This was generally due to the fact that God wished to change more than their name. It meant He wanted to change their identity, which ultimately led them to a place of discovering and fulfilling God's purpose for their lives.

Take Abram and Sarai as an example. God changed their names in the book of Genesis to Abraham and Sarah. The name Abraham means, "Father of a multitude," (Genesis 17:5) and Sarah means, "Mother of nations," (Genesis 17:15). God was letting them know that with the name change came a change of direction and a purpose beyond themselves. They were to pursue God's divine plan for their lives. It was more than simply a name change. For them, it also meant more diapers and baby strollers!

We see this same thing happen in Jacob's life. God changed his name to Israel (Genesis 32:28) and Simon became Peter (John 1:42). We also see people in the Bible attempt to change their names to reflect their circumstances. One such example comes to us in the first chapter of the Old Testament book of Ruth. Naomi, which means "beautiful," attempts to change her name to Mara, which means "bitter." This change comes after her husband dies, reflecting the change in her surroundings and the pain she felt.

Similar occurrences took place with Joseph in Genesis 41:45, Daniel in chapter 1:7, and Esther (Esther 2:7). In each case, whether God changed the name or an individual changed their own name, it reflected a change in their circumstances and surroundings. Their name change brought about a greater awareness of their life's meaning.

The second reason I knew God had spoken to me that morning was due to the strong sense of peace and clarity of His voice. In other words, God's Word and the Spirit of God were working together to ensure I would embrace what He was revealing to me. There was no confusion. God invited me to sit down and listen.

One of the lessons I've learned about God over the years is that He addresses us where we live. One could say I was used to having my name changed. My last name had changed three times up to this point. Each time was out of the pain of my family going through another divorce, abandonment, change of address, and deep hurt.

God was expressing this to me in a language I completely understood. Having my name changed wasn't foreign to me. God was asking me to glance out the rear-view mirror for just a moment, so that I would look out the windshield where He'd show me something greater on the road ahead.

I sat down on the steps leading up to the stage. It was one of those, "Speak, Lord, for your servant is listening," times in my life.

"I want to change your name from Rod to Rodney," He said.

I know, I know. I thought the same thing! As a matter of fact, I said what both you and I are thinking.

"Ummm, God…my name is Rodney," I whispered.

I'm so glad God is patient with us! He's willing to work through all the questions and times we don't get it. I wonder if God put His hand over His eyes, shook His head, and shouted, "Oy vey!"

God responded back, "People call you Rod. I'm changing it. Look up what Rodney means." And that was it.

Immediately I grabbed my things and headed to my office. This was before the days of smartphones or I would have simply looked it up. Yes, there was a time when they didn't exist! Believe me when I say I was eager to discover the meaning. I searched frantically through my bookshelves for a book on the meaning of names, only to come up short. After a few moments I noticed a dictionary sitting on my shelf.

Some of you reading this may have a difficult time understanding what I'm about to tell you. God not only knows what to say to us, and how to say it, but He also knows when and where. By speaking it to me at that moment He would also know that the only place I could go to find the meaning of Rodney that morning would be in a dictionary found in my office.

In case you're unaware, the dictionary has meanings of names in the back. Not all names are there, but quite a few are. Of course the chance that Rodney would be there was slim. I have problems finding my name on souvenir key rings, coffee mugs, or those small license plates that go on the back of your bicycle. Nevertheless, I searched through the dictionary, and there it was: Rodney.

Tears filled my eyes as I read the meaning of my name. I must have read it a dozen times in that moment. "Famous Admiral." Doesn't mean anything to you? Most likely not. I understand. You'd have to see what I saw staring at in the rearview mirror to grasp it. What I haven't told you is that my first three dads were in the Navy, each of them young sailors and low in rank. Most likely they held the rank of Seaman. That morning God continued to speak in a language I would understand, telling me I was no longer the son of a Seaman but I was now an Admiral. He had me glance through the mirror of my past to behold my future.

God has an incredible sense of humor. Remember, at the time of this name change I was a pastor in Nebraska. For those geologically challenged, Nebraska is located in the middle of the country. Just about dead center. About as far away from any ocean as you can get. Not exactly a hot spot for would-be Admirals. Where would I park my aircraft carrier or submarine? Although nothing changed in the natural, something had changed supernaturally, and the effects of that would soon be felt in my life. It was the same for Abraham and Sarah. It wasn't until later that the fruit of their name change showed itself. It was just the beginning.

But the story doesn't end here. A few years following my name change we found ourselves in the midst of transition to our next ministry assignment. We would be leaving the church where I had spent the last seven years praying in the aisle, under the balcony. On our final Sunday the church hosted a farewell celebration for us. The night was filled with hugs, fond memories being exchanged, and more than a few tears.

As the night drew to a close, one of the leaders in our church, who also worked in city government, handed me a large manila envelope. I pulled out a large certificate, and was suddenly overcome with an ocean of emotions. God was addressing me and once again speaking with His unique sense of humor. Proverbs 17:22 tells us laughter is good medicine! I don't think God would prescribe this type of medicine to us unless He also enjoyed a bit of it Himself. Inside the envelope was a certificate from the Governor of Nebraska. The certificate had my name on it, informing me I'd been commissioned to be an admiral in the Nebraska Navy! I have to be honest with you; I didn't know Nebraska had a Navy.

Revelation 2:17 mentions that one day, not too far away, everyone who has relationship with Jesus will receive a new name that only you will understand. Why a new name? It speaks of a new identity as you now find yourself engulfed in His full presence, transformed for His purposes, for all eternity.

But until that day, we are left here on earth to discover and fulfill our destiny. Often we can find our future by glancing out the mirror and remaining focused on what's ahead. In other words...there are times when we need to glance backwards in order to see forward.

As fate would have it, our next ministry assignment, now as an admiral in the navy, was in Grand Island, Nebraska! I would now have someplace to park my aircraft carrier!

CHAPTER NINE

WOULD YOU LIKE TO DANCE?

The mountains you encounter in life may be there so others can see how one casts them into the sea. (See Mark 11:23.)

I may be dating myself, but perhaps you've heard of the Sadie Hawkins dance. This annual bash took place while I attended high school in Nebraska. The gimmick behind the shindig is that the girls ask the guys they've been eyeballing during the school year. As you can imagine, there was quite a bit of scrambling, as the girls would finally get a chance to ask the guy of their dreams, rather than wait to be asked.

Over the years I'd become pretty good at planning ahead, carefully contemplating each detail from every angle. My intentional forecasting was solely meant for my own protection. The better I arranged something, the fewer surprises I had to navigate through. I'd determined early on in life that I had enough bombshells, and the fewer that caught me off guard the better. I'm also fairly creative. So I combined my creative flair and compulsive planning to craft a reason why I wouldn't be invited to the Sadie Hawkins jamboree.

My artistic strategy included making giant poster board sized signs to hang throughout the school. Hanging these signs throughout the school gave the appearance that I wanted girls to know they could call me for a date. At the same time it gave me a legitimate reason why no one called. I deliberately placed these enormous signs in front of every girls bathroom entrance throughout the school. I knew that the ladies would need to pass my signs at least a few times each day leading up to the festivities.

My artwork included my name, phone number and my availability for the evening. Any guesses as to how many invitations I received? Exactly. A big fat zero.

In all honesty I was somewhat relieved by this. I really didn't like dances and I'm not sure what I would have done had someone actually called. What I discovered about myself from this episode didn't occur to me until several years later. My attempt to gain a laugh from classmates was really a sign indicating my own insecurities. I'd done this so I wouldn't have to tell anyone why I wasn't at the dance. Going overboard with the project guaranteed my protection from additional rejection.

For years I'd been dancing around feelings of abandonment in my life. It was in God's grace and love for me that He began prepping me for a couple of surgeries on my soul in order to bring the much-needed transformation in my life.

In November of 1988, following our first ministry assignment in Nebraska, my wife, Kim, and I moved to serve as youth pastors in New Jersey. The church sat directly across the street from Princeton University and was surrounded by the allure of a quaint university community. Unique shops, with large window displays filled with exclusive and expensive items, lined the sidewalks of Nassau Street. Students from all over the world walked along those same streets as they made their way to classes.

Our daughter, Lindsay, was just 20 months old, and Kim was pregnant with our second daughter, Bethany. She was born in May of 1989, and later our son Michael would claim New Jersey as his home in September of 1992.

To say that New Jersey was remarkably different from Nebraska would be quite the understatement. The pace of life and traffic, the crowds, the diversity, the cost of living, the culture, referring to pop as "soda," well…everything was a dramatic change. Our new assignment took us out of our comfort zone in many ways, the next step in the continuing change that would be a part of my life. This variation would in many ways determine the extent of healing needed in my life.

Deep wounds were opened that I'd attempted to cover over. What I needed was radical surgery, due to completely ignoring, or even being unaware of, the pain I'd attempted to push down in my life. Most people don't like dealing with their past because it ushers in the ugly emotions that were born in pain, guilt, and shame. But it's through those earlier excruciating experiences that God seemed to do His best work. We often fail to realize that God is continually working behind the scenes to bring health to our life. His aim isn't to change our outward behavior as much as it is to transform our inward character.

"And I am certain that God, who began the good work within you, will continue his work until it is finally finished on the day when Christ Jesus returns" (Philippians 1:6).

My initial response to God's call to New Jersey was only a part of this soul renovation. I was a youth pastor and was doing my best to reach teens with the message of God's love, and encourage them. What I didn't know was that God was simultaneously reaching out to me, bringing me the same message. Yes, answering His call to serve in ministry was part of God's plan for my life, but His ultimate desire was to see me whole. God positions us in order to prepare our hearts for a life altering makeover.

Perhaps this is the reason I understand the story of Jonah so much. Outwardly, we see God positioning Jonah to go to Nineveh. Jonah was to tell the people about God. What we read in the four chapters of the book is the story of a man who needed surgery.

We see how Jonah ran from God. Later we see how he wanted to die. Isn't this a picture of many people's lives? They run from the God who loves them, and then later feel hopeless. I relate to Jonah. Certainly God could have chosen a hundred others to go to Nineveh. I believe He chose

Jonah in order to bring healing in his life. What we view as God moving us may be Him positioning us for internal change.

From our first days on the East Coast, I loved everything about it. I enjoyed the students, the church, the community, and the new ministry challenge. Additionally, I would be part of a pastoral staff with three other pastors. This came in quite handy for golf outings and two-on-two basketball games. We prayed together and played together. I learned a great deal while on staff, but the core lesson was only just beginning.

Four years into our time in New Jersey things began to change in the atmosphere. It wasn't an overnight difference, but rather one that was drawn out over several months. Confidential phone conversations, closed-door meetings, and abysmal rumors were now taking place. Questions arose regarding the pastor's integrity. I was dumbfounded. My pastor had become a mentor/father figure to me. He was brilliant and charismatic. I relished our enriching conversations in his home and office. He cared for me and my family in many ways.

I recall on one particular day he stopped by with a new kitchen table and chairs because we didn't have one. He even stayed around to help set it up. He loved my family, which is what every youth pastor wants from their lead pastor. We were invited to his house for holidays since we had no other family in the area. He dedicated two of our children to the Lord. He was more than a boss, he was a friend. He was also quite the jokester. Needless to say we had a great deal of fun together.

For example, I vividly recall preaching on a Sunday night, followed by an altar response time. With the music playing and people praying, I decided to step out in faith and lead in singing. Do I need to remind you of my fifth-grade choir episode?

People were connecting with God, and I was leading in song as they prayed. Well…all but one. My pastor! Sometime during my singing he'd jumped on another microphone to help me in my efforts. After about

15 minutes in this time of prayer, I turned around to observe the people praying, and I saw my pastor lying on the floor, laughing. I guess I was singing off key and didn't realize it. We laugh about it to this day.

As time progressed, tensions grew between staff members, and more business-like relationships began to develop. I hated that these things we going on. We grew from a staff that enjoyed one another to one that simply endured ministry and each other. I looked up to and respected the other leaders. I loved our students. I loved the church.

The mounting tensions finally came to a head one weekend. The service went as planned; it was another great time of worship and a wonderful message. As was the norm, I stood in the back shaking hands, hugging necks, and doing my best to encourage people. The family then headed home to enjoy lunch before returning to church for our Sunday evening service. That afternoon I ventured outside to do some much-needed yard work. Halfway through my mowing I noticed Kim standing outside with the phone in her hand, waving me to come in. I turned the mower off. Funny how one moment can instantaneously alter your life forever.

"Pastor wants to speak with you," she said.

I responded, "Ask him if it would be all right for me to call him when I'm finished."

"He wants to speak with you right away."

This wasn't typical. In over four years my pastor had never called me on a Sunday afternoon. He'd never asked to talk with me right away, either. I was always able to call him later. I walked to the phone, thinking this must be something very serious. I began sorting through a mental checklist of everything that had happened that week. I wondered if I'd overlooked something or if I had done something wrong. As I checked the final item from my list, I found myself standing on the front porch. Kim handed the phone to me.

"I need you to cover the service tonight," he uttered.

"Sure," I said. "Aren't you going to be there? What about the other guys? Can I ask why you're wanting me to handle the service?"

I was just the youth pastor. The others are associates, and more qualified and do a better job.

"You're going to find out later anyway so I'll tell you now," he said. "There's been meeting called. I'll be in this meeting with the board members and the other two staff members. It was me."

It's not important what the issue was. Except that it was the sharp blade of the surgeon's knife beginning its cut into my soul. There was no time for anesthetic. I don't remember handing the phone back to Kim or finishing the lawn. I don't remember cleaning up or driving to church. It was happening again. My blue skies had once again turned cloudy and dark. I was riding what seemed to be an eternal, never-ending roller coaster of failures, disappointments, and continual abandonment.

While I conducted the service, my pastor was being asked to resign his position and evacuate the building within the week. I left the church that evening feeling like I'd been pushed off a bridge, falling but without a bungee cord or any landing pad in site. The following week was a complete blur. Suddenly it was the next Sunday and the pastor of our church, and my mentor and friend, was standing before the congregation announcing his resignation.

Over the next couple of months I cried out to the Lord much the same way David must have when he wrote some of the Psalms. I was searching for answers in the midst of a million questions. I was emotionally shattered and didn't know whom to trust. After all, I was the only staff or board member not included in the closed-door meeting. Not that I wanted to be included, but it left me on the outs. Who could I trust? What would happen to the church? Who had been plotting for how long? Who was right? Once again, I'd been left empty. Had the Church abandoned me as well?

"Save me, O God, for the floodwaters are up to my neck. Deeper and deeper I sink into the mire; I can't find a foothold. I am in deep water, and the floods overwhelm me. I am exhausted from crying for help; my throat is parched. My eyes are swollen with weeping, waiting for my God to help me" (Psalm 69:1-3).

As I sought the Lord over the next couple of months, He began to speak more clearly to me than I ever remember Him doing. It was as loud as an audible voice without any sound. He was shouting to my soul. His shouts were the stitches used to sew the deep incision. Sadly, I had allowed the ease of life to lull me to sleep in my relationship with God. The resignation of my pastor was an abrupt sounding alarm to my slumber. I found myself spinning in a whirlpool of emotions.

God told me, through a sequence of intimate conversations, that we would be moving and that we would have an answer as to the location the first of November. A few months later, on the last Saturday of October, I received an unexpected phone call from a close friend in Nebraska. He was now the lead pastor of the church Kim and I had begun our ministry in, and he was calling to offer us a position. Six months later we packed our things and made the trip west.

God tirelessly works to produce the needed healing in our lives, even when we're completely oblivious. While we're busy making a living, taking care of our families, making repairs on our homes, running errands, trying to exercise more, and attending church, He attempts to make us more like Him. This restorative work often reveals itself to us in moments where we least expect it.

"So all of us who have had that veil removed can see and reflect the glory of the Lord. And the Lord—who is the Spirit—makes us more and more like him as we are changed into his glorious image" (2 Corinthians 3:18).

My experience was part of God's purpose in moving us to New Jersey. A state lined with turnpikes, parkways, toll roads, and jughandles. Not the greener pastures of Psalm 23. New Jersey became the operating table God placed me on in order to make a deeper laceration. His skilled hands delicately reached into my raw soul to begin the procedure. Ironically called the Garden State, this season in my life served to awaken me to the harsh north winds of winter meant to produce cleansing, character, and courage.

"Awake, north wind! Rise up, south wind! Blow on my garden and spread its fragrance all around. Come into your garden, my love; taste its finest fruits" (Song of Solomon 4:16).

Our lives are the garden. God was blowing the much-needed, but often-uncomfortable, cold north winds over my soul. He does this so that the plot of land that is our soul becomes rich with the finest fruit. These seasons of intense and multi-directional winds serve to help us reach our full potential. Like the bride in Song of Solomon 4:16, I had both the north and south winds blowing on my life. Unlike the Bride, I didn't ask for those winds.

Why does God do surgery on us when we didn't check ourselves into the hospital to begin with? I believe it's because of God's heart of compassion for us. He is devoted to us. He longs for us to walk in freedom from our past, our failures, our sin, and the shame that often accompanies them. He knows when we need the surgery. He pierces into us to remove what's keeping us from experiencing life-changing freedom. The question is whether we'll accept this as His hand of grace doing the work. Too many times I've pushed His hand aside.

I wasn't aware of God performing an operation on my soul. I also didn't realize that this period in my life was only the pre-op, and that the real work would begin to show itself in the years following our move. Just when we're thoroughly convinced the operation is over we find ourselves back on the surgical table. The continual work of His Spirit is evidence of your value to Him. Your value was never just for eternity in heaven, but also for the present. As I look back on this I recognize the depth of healing needed in my life. I saw the grace-filled compassion the Lord chose to take in the process. I'm extremely grateful for the subtle sensitivity of the Spirit's work.

We arrived back in Bellevue, Nebraska, in April of 1994. This was the community I'd moved to during my ninth-grade year—where I'd graduated high school, and where I first began attending church while a teenager. I never thought I'd be back, but God had more surgery to do. He felt it necessary to bring me back to Nebraska for the next procedure. Perhaps He brought me back to a familiar place because the surgery would be more intense. It was as if God was retracing my past to help me navigate the present and regain my future. Once again, the operation would involve a staff member I'd grown to admire.

During my first year on staff I'd developed a friendship with one of the associate pastors of the church. I'd barely known him prior to joining the team, but now that I was on staff I found myself getting to know and trust him. We worked on projects together and shared in lunches. He was well liked in the church, a gifted communicator, and always seemed to conduct himself in a professional manner.

About 18 months after our arrival I was walking through the church parking lot when a couple of young men from the church hesitantly approached me. They'd been struggling with information regarding a staff member, when they happened to cross paths with me. I've learned over the years that God often seems to arrange things backstage. Then, when we least expect it, He pulls back the curtain. Surprise! I happened to be standing on the stage when He pulled it back that day.

Without going into specifics regarding what they'd seen, my co-worker (and friend) had been seen by these two conducting himself in an unethical manner. A few days later I found myself in a meeting with the lead pastor and his wife, and the staff member and his wife. This time I was smack dab in the middle of it. I much prefer being on the outs. By the end of the encounter the associate had been asked to step down from his position. Once again, someone I'd looked up to and respected had been removed.

I walked out the door and headed directly for the sanctuary of the church. It wasn't that I thought about going to the sanctuary, rather, my feet just seemed to carry me there. I stepped through the doors and emotionally vomited. Every emotion inside spewed out in that one moment. Tears gushed from my eyes. My body shook. Pain from my past that had nothing to do with the current situation was making its way through my cries. I hurt. The surgeon's knife sliced deep.

Answering God's assignment seems to be secondary to God transforming our lives. Scripture is clear. God wants us to live an abundant life (John 10:10). The problem is our understanding of that verse may be very different from God's meaning. We often think of abundant life as having all the external things we need to bring us happiness. Abundance for many means a wonderful spouse, new house and car, nice clothes, a clean bill of health, money in a mutual fund, the latest technological devices, a great job, no stress, and a faithful dog that doesn't shed.

God's definition of abundance is different. An abundant life means healthy emotions and thoughts, and a wholesome, growing spiritual life so we can answer His call. It's the latter that truly brings glory to God, not the former. Abundance is found in the wealth of God's compassion, not the lavishness of things. It's the richness of vigorous relationships, not the excess of wealth, that makes a man rich. Poverty isn't the lack of money, but the surplus of loneliness.

The less we understand regarding God's love, the more hollow our lives feel and look to those around us. Others see it, and we don't. We find ourselves walking through the mire of our past, unable to keep in step with God and His plan for our lives. We slowly lose hope and live in a world of misery when we refuse to understand the depth of God's grace for us.

We lose control—we become fearful, critical, and angry. Often anger rages in our lives because the world around us is shaking. This described my life. I'd spent most of my life questioning my identity, the worth I brought to others, and the purpose for my life. My life was spent living day to day rather than living each day understanding and helping others experience God's favor. You can't be of great help to others when you're struggling to find value yourself.

Fortunately we serve a God who's both persistent and patient. He spent years by my side, slowly inching me forward toward the healing He desperately craved for my life. He invites me to dance.

"You have turned my mourning into joyful dancing" (Psalm 30:11).

But it was my Father in heaven who held me close while we danced across the floor of life. I experienced the ache of disillusionment and abandonment. I needed to hear the music again. The harder I sought a father figure, the more bankrupt I became. God wanted to be my Father. He desperately longs to be yours. It wasn't until I went through these two incidents that I fully realized the father figure I'd been searching for my entire life was found only in my Father in heaven. You may think just because I was in ministry that I would know this. I'm a slow learner.

People often ask how I could see or embrace or love God as a father figure when all around me were terrible examples of fatherhood. I've seen a father abandon me. I've lived through the brutal assassination of a father. I've seen an alcoholic and abusive father, and an adulterous one. I've seen spiritual father figures tragically fall from the pedestal I'd placed them atop.

My response to their question is always the same: God is the only Father who has never left me. He's still alive today and for eternity. He's kind and compassionate, never abusive. He has been and remains faithful. He is and will forever be my all in all. Though the surgery He performs stings, it's meant to revive us. Soul surgery is the beginning of a revival that ushers in a new you.

"This means that anyone who belongs to Christ has become a new person. The old life is gone; a new life has begun" (2 Corinthians 5:17).

Perhaps you've been under the knife of His Spirit more times than you can count. What you don't realize is that God, the Father, is resurrecting you. If you're like me, then some of those times you weren't even aware you were being opened up. May I encourage you in this? Allow God to carefully make the incision. He does His best work when we rest in Him.

Now…take a deep breath and start counting backwards. 100….99…98…

CHAPTER TEN

MY FIRST DAY OF SCHOOL

Don't allow the dark moments of your past to thwart the bright encounters to come in your future.

"Doesn't he see everything I do and every step I take?" (Job 31:4).

We tend to view our lives through the lens of our past experiences. Too often our history has far too great an influence on our lives. At times it prevents us from becoming the person God has destined us to become.

It was my first day of kindergarten. My mom was working full time and my siblings were taken care of by a babysitter. We lived in San Francisco, a city built on hills.

My mom had carefully prepared me for my first day as a student by walking me from our house to the entrance of the school a few days before school started. I'd have to navigate my journey on my own, as my mom would leave prior to my trek. I don't remember it being that far from our house but what I do remember is that just before coming to the school I would have to climb a ginormous number of steps. The adventurous walk would take me past several homes, up a number of stairs, and across a street to where my learning would begin.

I remember hiking down the street and coming to the bottom of the steps. I stood stationary for just a moment before placing my foot on the first stair. Reaching the top and taking my first footstep onto the level ground above woke me to the reality of the outside world. I paused motionless, staring at my new school.

Children and parents, teachers and administrators, and cars and buses were between the school and me. None of these were present the day my mom took me on our dress rehearsal. I was, at that moment, a terrified little boy. That was as far as I got that day. I quickly turned, feet barely touching the steps on the way down, and sprinted home.

Later that morning my mom called the school to make sure I'd arrived. Of course, they had no record of me entering the school that day. I can only imagine the thoughts that went through my mom's mind that day as she realized her first-born son never made it to school. She must have been wracked with guilt that she wasn't able to see her son safely on his first day. Frantically pulling into the driveway that morning she found me sitting on the front porch of our tiny home.

I didn't have a dad on my first day of school—no one to tell me it would be all right. I loved my mom but I needed a dad's strength and confidence as I encountered new quests in life. Exploits that would be needed to reach the destiny and purpose for my life. This leads me to a set of steps I had to take in life that proved to be much more challenging than my first day of kindergarten.

The chapel had been beautifully decorated. The guests had been warmly greeted and seated. Smiles were everywhere. Wedding music played ever so softly in the background. Pictures scrolled on the giant screens hanging just above the platform of the church chapel. The bridesmaids and groomsmen began to saunter down the aisle. It was my daughter's wedding. The two of us patiently waited in the hallway, just outside the packed chapel. I say patiently but I'm sure Bethany was feeling anything but patient, as she waited to be forever united to her future husband. Personally, I had no problem waiting a few more moments…hours…years, longer before giving her up.

If you take time to look back on your life you realize that God was patiently working His plan in you each step. Perhaps you didn't notice it initially but it doesn't negate the fact that He was walking with you. We encounter difficult seasons in our lives and question the purpose behind those moments.

Why do bad things happen to good people? We wonder if all the pain in our lives will one day have a purpose this side of eternity. I've looked back on my own life, having had four fathers, wondering if my pain could somehow bring healing and meaning to my life.

In other words: Is there purpose in pain? If you've read this far, then I imagine you're wondering the same thing. I'm in no way suggesting that God brings us pain to give us purpose. But I believe God allows moments of hurt in order to keep us from harm. Every person experiences the sting of suffering. I'm simply asking if it's possible for God to take what the enemy of our soul meant for evil and turn it into something beautiful.

For me it came down to learning how to lead from a place of healing rather than leading from a position of hurt.

If you were to ask me the one prayer I've prayed more than any prayer, it would be to be a good father. I often felt so inadequate in this role. I'm sure you can understand why. At the expense of being overly dramatic, I didn't have a dad to walk me up the steps to school that day. That wedding day I wasn't sure if I had been or could be a good enough father to walk my daughter down a level aisle.

Some of my biggest regrets are the missed opportunities I had to be a good father. After sharing my story on countless occasions, people have questioned how I could be such a good father with all the bad examples I've had in my life. I certainly don't feel that I've been a good father. Rather, I suspect that I've blown it more than I'd care to admit.

"For our present troubles are small and won't last very long. Yet they produce for us a glory that vastly outweighs them and will last forever! So we don't look at the troubles we can see now; rather, we fix our gaze on things that cannot be seen. For the things we see now will soon be gone, but the things we cannot see will last forever" (2 Corinthians 4:17-18).

Sadly, many people painfully travel through life without contemplating any great purpose from their pain. Instead, they remain tragically absorbed in their own pain, hurts, and heartache. The truly heartbreaking issue isn't whether any of us will experience abandonment, questions of self-worth, or shameful acts. The question for each of us is whether or not we'll discover a way to use it to fuel the vision God has for us.

Many go through life grabbing at every offense they can, convincing themselves that it's everyone else's fault they're the way they are. If I had a dad, I would have made it up those steps that day! Where was he? As a result, I end up carrying a weighted backpack full of offenses into every future relationship and situation in my life. It's no wonder I end up turning around and heading back down the stairs to sit on the front porch, alone.

You see, as soon as I stop blaming or hating, I'm forced to deal with my past. I'm brought to a place where I'm asked to let go of the offenses and forgive. Until my past is dealt with, I'm unable to fully forge ahead and embrace my purpose. This truth is one that has taken me several years to comprehend and implement in my life, and it once again revealed itself to me in a great way on the day of my daughter's wedding.

The steps down the aisle seemed to go faster than the speed of light, and the entire ceremony was over before I could blink. By the time I could catch my breath the minister declared, "You may kiss the bride." It was over. My daughter had a husband and would spend the remainder of her life with another man. For her first 21 years I was the man in her life and was responsible for her. Now she would be under the care of another. (He's a wonderful man, by the way!)

The two of them had met eight years prior to the wedding, so I'd known her husband for several years. Griffin came from a great family, with his dad being a fellow minister and personal friend. I'd traveled in ministry with Griffin's father, Mark, and knew him to be a passionate follower and gifted minister of Christ.

Just one year after spending a week traveling together, Griffin's father unexpectedly and suddenly passed away from a heart attack. Griffin was one of four sons and just 15 years old at the time.

"Who now gives this woman to be married to this man?" asked the minister.

"Her mother and I," I replied.

I was handing off my daughter to a young man who'd lost his dad while a teenager. I realize I'm not the first dad to give his daughter to someone who had gone through such a tragic situation. I offer this to you showing that in the midst of my own pain, God was granting me divine purpose. I was to become more than a father-in-law to young Griffin. Somehow I was to love as a dad who understood the pain of having lost a father. It wasn't my place to take the place of Griffin's dad, for no one could do this. But God lovingly placed me in his life to come alongside. The old adage held true: I wasn't losing a daughter; I was gaining a son.

Years later my oldest son, and third in line to the throne, married a beautiful Columbian woman. Micaela was raised in a culture where family meant everything. Her dad was also a pastor of a church before suffering multiple strokes that left him needing constant medical attention. He was placed in a rehabilitation center just outside of Miami. Micaela was one of four daughters living with her mom. This was partly due to the family culture she was raised in and the need to combine incomes in order to make ends meet.

Following my son's church ceremony, the wedding party loaded into vehicles to head to the rehabilitation center for a private ceremony with Micaela's father. He deserved to see his daughter married. As you can imagine, it was a very emotional service for everyone in attendance. There were many tears, a few laughs, and countless hugs. This was the first and only time I would ever have the privilege of seeing her father. A few months following the ceremony he entered heaven.

Two of my three in-laws were now without a father—fathers taken way too soon. This sometimes feels as if God is allowing me to be a father to more than just my own children. I now refer to my son- and daughter-in-law as my son- and daughter-in-love. I know it's a bit corny, but true. Both have graciously allowed me into their lives in profound ways.

As different as Griffin and Micaela are, I think it's more than coincidence that both of their fathers were ministers. Griffin came from a family of four boys, and Micaela came from a family of four girls. Yet as unique as their backgrounds were, God chose to bring them into our family. He also chose to bring me into theirs. I believe one reason for this is to bring restoration—not just their own personal healing, but mine as well. He's the God of second chances.

If I'd chosen to continue blaming my dads, or even hating them, I would miss out on the opportunity to be a dad to those God brings me. My value in this life was becoming clearer to me each day. No longer was I to live thinking my worth was that of a five-dollar bet or one-night stand. I had value to two young people who needed a father figure in their lives. I cringe to think what my future would have looked like had I remained bitter or unforgiving.

Did you ever read the story in the Bible about a guy named Joseph? He had every right to hold a tremendous grudge against his brothers. They considered killing him, only to later sell him as a slave and then lie to their father about his fate. For the next several years they lived with the knowledge of all they'd done to their brother, but felt comfortable enough to not mention it.

Joseph could have easily grown embittered and incensed. Others would have counseled him to destroy the lives of his brothers. He had every right not to forgive. Joseph encountered several detours in life but years later found himself second-in-command to Pharaoh. His role now positioned him to make life and death decisions. Think about that for a moment. We too make life and death decisions to each person we meet in life.

We see that the land Joseph oversaw was experiencing a severe famine. It was at this moment his brothers show up to purchase food. They entered the court but didn't recognize Joseph. Remember, approximately 17 years had passed and they were convinced he was now dead. The last person they ever expected to see would be their own brother, in charge of a nation's food supply.

The ugly reality is that pain from a family member is so destructive. His 10 brothers turned their back on Joseph. Rather than retaliate, Joseph gave his brothers food and opened Pharaoh's court to them. He realized he had a greater purpose in the midst of the pain he'd suffered. He came to understand that God had been working through his life in order to establish him in a place of honor. Joseph's integrity led him to a place of influence in the lives of others. It was from this position that he was able to help several families, including his own.

We see this truth went far beyond Joseph's own life. There's a legacy we leave for future generations when we embrace the purposes in our lives. Engage the pain, not to hold onto it, but to see how God turns it into life-altering purpose.

I love the story of Joseph. Don't forget he was a real person who experienced extreme physical abuse and emotional pain. What I find fascinating about his life is that he remained focused on God throughout all of it. Approximately 15 years after being sold by his brothers into slavery he finds himself, having been falsely accused, in prison with the king's baker and cup-bearer. God directs our steps. There are no coincidences with God. Joseph remains steadfast in character. Take a look at how he initiates a conversation one morning with his two prison buddies.

"When Joseph saw them the next morning, he noticed that they both looked upset. 'Why do you look so worried today?' he asked them" (Genesis 40:6-7).

Joseph doesn't come in complaining about his own condition. Rather, he notices the baker and cup-bearer appear to be upset. After 15 painful years of abandonment, Joseph continues to notice and support others. He's concerned for them. He remains unselfish. I want to be that kind of individual! Joseph makes living life about aiding others. Joseph had no guarantee that helping the two convicts would help him in his own situation. He did it out of genuine concern.

Now years later we realize the scope of God's leading in Joseph's life. He's reunited with his brothers and father. He's married and remains second-in-command.

"Joseph named his older son Manasseh, for he said, 'God has made me forget all my troubles and everyone in my father's family.' Joseph named his second son Ephraim, for he said, 'God has made me fruitful in this land of my grief' " (Genesis 41:51-52).

Joseph names his two sons Manasseh and Ephraim. The meanings of their names reflect Joseph's heart in the midst of all he encountered in life. He chooses to forget and forgive, and realizes that God has made his life fruitful as a result of that decision, even in the land of his grief.

The greatest fruit is often grown in the darkest valley. Pain with purpose comes when we're willing to forgive and trust God in the tough times in our lives. The seeds of forgiveness we plant eventually grow into a crop of fruitfulness!

Later, as Joseph's father Jacob is near death, he asks Joseph to bring his sons to him so he can bless them. By rights, Manasseh should have received the greater blessing due to the fact that he was the first-born of the two. But while Joseph bowed his head, his father switched his hands, giving Ephraim the greater blessing. Joseph became upset at this and then we read Jacob's response.

"But his father refused. 'I know, my son; I know,' he replied. 'Manasseh will also become a great people, but his younger brother will become even greater. And his descendants will become a multitude of nations.' " (Genesis 48:19).

I believe Jacob's richer blessing was on Ephraim for the following reason. Recall what Ephraim means: fruitful. In other words, it was Jacob proclaiming there would be great fruit as a result of Joseph forgiving his brothers. Many people find the path of bitterness easier to travel than the road of forgiveness. Joseph, having traveled this arduous road of forgiveness, meant that his life would leave an enduring legacy long after he passed away. The greater blessing would show itself in the fruit of Joseph's life, because he chose to forgive.

Wouldn't it be nice to see down life's road, knowing ahead of time that things would be grandiose and that everyone would love us? Not really. Think about it for a moment. If we knew that by making certain decisions life would be better, most would choose to take that road. In the end, however, it would be said of us that we did it because it served to benefit us.

What if, instead, we determined to show kindness, love, goodness, peace, faithfulness, patience, joy, self-control, and gentleness to others—regardless of circumstances? It would be said of us that we loved through our pain, with little or no guarantee that things would be better. We simply chose to live by faith that God was with us each step. Our lasting legacy comes when we choose to forgive. You're never more like Jesus than when you choose to forgive in the midst of your own suffering. This is the message of the cross.

The fruit of Jesus' life continues to impact the lives of people even 2,000 years later. His Father chose to bring great fruit to the life of His Son, Jesus, because He chose to live a life of forgiveness. He chose to embrace the suffering needed to leave a legacy. Jesus experienced abandonment from His Father, but lived completely abandoned to serving and loving others. All with no real guarantee that others will respond to His love for them.

Imagine Jesus not forgiving because of the pain and abandonment He felt. You and I would have no hope. In the center of His anguish He had purpose—His life given to see you and me live a fruitful life. His pain had purpose: you and me.

I had to come face to face with the reality that I *could* be a good dad. My past had shaped me to think that this could never be the case. The examples I had in my life left me questioning if there was such a thing. Could I ever be the dad I dreamed of having? Would I be able to bring the kind of value I would want for my own children? These are questions that plagued me on a consistent basis. I'd allowed my past to influence my present, which ultimately would outline my future.

"Don't copy the behavior and customs of this world, but let God transform you into a new person by changing the way you think. Then you will learn to know God's will for you, which is good and pleasing and perfect" (Romans 12:2).

In order for me to become all that God had for me, I had to allow Him to transform the way I thought, the way I lived, the way I loved. Each day is an opportunity to renew my mind by understanding God's love for me, and the value He's placed on my life.

May the God of Heaven give you tremendous grace to take that first step up the steep staircase. The tremendous news is you don't walk alone. Your Father is walking to school with you.

CHAPTER ELEVEN

ARE YOU AFRAID OF THE DARK?

"The great illusion of leadership is to think that man can be led out of the desert by someone who has never been there." *~Henri Nouwen,* The Wounded Healer

Moses experienced it. Joseph underwent it. David faced it. Paul felt it. Jesus walked it.

In absolutely no way am I comparing myself to any of these men, except to say that I've also experienced it. And so have you. What is it you ask? It's the season in your life when you find yourself walking in the desert. It's the days, weeks, months, and even years when you feel as if your prayers don't have enough faith behind them to reach the ceiling above you. Those moments when you feel like you're the tackling dummy for the Oakland Raiders practice session. Everyone on the team is running toward you at full speed, ready to inflict life-threatening damage. You stand on life's field with no fight left. Not caring, and hoping—begging — for this season to be over.

When I was in third grade we lived in Paradise Valley, Arizona. Our home was in a brand new development, directly across the street from a desert. Most days my brother and I would spend countless hours playing on the hot playground. We built forts, created an elaborate system of roads through the sands to push our toy cars, and imagined we were explorers discovering a new land. We crossed paths with snakes and scorpions on many expeditions. I was even stung on my knee by a scorpion, followed immediately by a trip to the doctor. Occasionally, as darkness fell, we would make our way across our street, to the edge of the desert, daring each other to walk into the darkness that settled on our playground.

Off in the distance we would hear the howls of coyotes, which added a whole new dimension to the already scary nighttime triple-dog dare. One at a time, we would begin the walk into the night sand. We cautiously approached each step as if it would be our last. With each stride we were blanketed with the dark night and met with the chilling howls of a coyote that seemed to be only a few feet from us. It's amazing how vivid a third- and first-grader's imagination can be when met with utter blackness.

There are seasons in our lives when God calls us to the desert…at night…afraid…feeling alone. We stand poised at the edge, but rather than someone daring us to walk into the deserts of darkness and uncertainty, we're led there, with the terrifying howls as our background music. Our imagination conjures pictures of us as the main course for a coyote, and we convince ourselves that we'll forever be lost in the sands of a black hole.

"Remember how the LORD your God led you through the wilderness for these forty years, humbling you and testing you to prove your character, and to find out whether or not you would obey his commands" (Deuteronomy 8:2).

Yes, God leads us into the desert to humble us, test us, and see how obedient we are to His commands. Of course, He already knows how obedient we are, but He does this for us to discover the level of our own obedience. Will we continue to listen to Him? Will we trust Him? Love? Follow? What I've found is that these questions are much easier to answer from the comfort of our couch, during the daylight hours, across the street from the desert. They confront the makeup of our souls at a whole different level when we stand with our toes in the sand, unable to see the wild animals lurking beyond.

My brother would cautiously sink his feet into the sand. One step. A second one. A third. Pause. Scanning the horizon. Turning around to see if I was still behind him. A fourth. Now turning his ear toward the night sky to listen for the movements of creatures. Lifting his foot for the next, only to quickly turn and run back to the safe haven of the lit, paved road. The mark had been set. It was now my turn.

I never told my brother this but I always considered him much braver than me in every category of life. I was the oldest brother, and had to live up to the Braver Big Brother Code, that had been established centuries before. I couldn't let him see me scared, nor could I allow him to beat me. To do either would mean turning in my Big Brother Card. The balance of the universe was at stake. It was at this point that I'd offer some excuse as to why I wouldn't be able to take my turn, or suggest that it was time to go home. After all, I may not have been the most courageous, but I was savvier in my thinking.

In 2015 I found myself without a job for the second time in a year. This set me on the edge of the wilderness. Uncertain steps would have to be taken. Moves I had never taken prior to this. It was now time to travel farther into the gritty sand. How would we make it financially? How would I go about finding another position? How far would we have to move from family? I had never had to look for a ministry opportunity. In the past, God had always opened a position prior to me leaving the current one.

Fortunately, I had a few speaking engagements lined up to help us financially through the next several months. Financial security was only part of the journey, however. Like most men, I found much of my identity and worth in my work—my ministry.

God was testing me. Perhaps having these speaking arrangements would help me stay centered on serving, and not my circumstances. I wouldn't have to deal emotionally with the pain of it. What I didn't realize was that I was still standing on the edge of the desert. I hadn't yet encountered the howls of the coyotes or the ambiguity that waited ahead.

My annual physical came in March, and some blood work came back abnormal. My doctor didn't seem too concerned with the readings; he just wanted to keep an eye on it. Over the next couple of months my results continued to worsen with no apparent explanation. I felt good. I was exercising and trying to eat right. Simply put, there was no explanation for the continual decline.

Fast forward to June. Still without a job, I was told I needed to see a kidney specialist because my kidneys were failing. The only date the specialists could see me was during one of the youth camps where I was scheduled to speak. I called the leader to let him know I'd have to cancel my trip. This would be a difficult call for me, as I hated to put him in this situation. Little did I know I would have to make this same call to three other camps. All the income we'd counted on to help us through the summer was now gone. Financial guarantees, good health, and job guarantees were slowly slipping through my fingers. The more tightly I held my fingers together, the more the sands of security slithered through.

Step one into the desert. In July I had surgery. This would mean that my kidneys would not have to work so hard, allowing them to function at greater capacity. By this time my kidney function was at 25 percent. Stage four kidney failure. I entered the hospital on a Monday for the surgery, and would be home on Tuesday. One week of limited lifting and movement and then back to a normal life. Or so I thought.

Step two. Now both feet in the sand. My discharge from the hospital came on Tuesday and Kim drove me home as scheduled. The next morning I began experiencing pain in my leg, and by Thursday I was in the emergency room with what ended up being a blood clot that had developed from the surgery. I was given a blood thinner and sent back home.

Step three. The following Monday I was seen by my surgeon for my week check-up. After the appointment we headed home for what we believed would be the end of this difficulty, and life would return to normal. This wasn't the case, however, as Monday night we were back in the emergency room for the second time in five days. I was scheduled for another surgery the next morning.

Once again the surgery went well but I had to stay in the hospital a bit longer to make sure I would heal correctly this time. I had been losing blood due to the surgery and being on blood thinners, so I needed a unit of blood. One doctor said, "You're dancing between raindrops." My body couldn't adequately heal because my blood wouldn't clot due to the thinners. But I needed the thinners due to the clot.

Now, with coyotes howling, step four. Finally, I was released on Sunday morning after spending seven days in the hospital. We drove home praying that this would be the end, only to return to the emergency room that night. It was our third emergency room visit in just over a week, and would turn out to be our third—and then fourth—surgery in a three-week span. I was never in great physical pain but the emotional weight of uncertainty was as excruciating as any physical pain I could imagine. I was slowly sinking in the sands of doubt.

We returned to the ninth floor of the hospital following surgery, with the nurses shocked to see us again. What should have been a simple procedure, and one-night stay, turned into three weeks of multiple visits, surgeries, doctor appointments, sponge baths, hospital stays, and backless gowns. We were definitely being humbled, tested, and challenged to trust God with healing, finances, and faith. We were now standing fully immersed in the darkness of a wilderness we were completely unfamiliar with.

Our third hospital stay proved to be our final one. It took us three or four nights before we were able to fully rest in our own beds. We found ourselves waking throughout the night, wondering if there would be another emergency room visit, another doctor visit, another surgery, another carb-loaded hospital meal. Thankfully there was only one more small procedure a few months later. Following the procedure they discovered I no longer had a blood clot and wouldn't need a blood thinner anymore. Kim and I were extremely grateful for what God had done over the four months.

I don't know if you ever question God on why He allows certain things to take place. I had several questions during my three hospital stays. It wasn't until after the final stay that I was reminded of this verse.

"All praise to God, the Father of our Lord Jesus Christ. God is our merciful Father and the source of all comfort. He comforts us in all our troubles so that we can comfort others. When they are troubled, we will be able to give them the same comfort God has given us. For the more we suffer for Christ, the more God will shower us with his comfort through Christ" (2 Corinthians 1:3-5).

He comforts us in our moments so that we can comfort others in theirs! To focus on my pain and circumstances guarantees I miss out on being a blessing to others. I had experienced God's grace and compassion in tremendous ways. It was now my purpose to bring comfort to others. My purpose during this time wasn't to stand behind a pulpit to preach to the masses, but rather to lie in a hospital bed and pray with the one.

You see, I had four different roommates during my hospital stays. There are times when our pain reveals aspects of our purpose. I prayed with these men and encouraged them in the midst of the situation they were facing. I discovered a couple of the men faced much greater challenges than me. My work was to do what Jesus would do in this same situation. In some extremely small way I understood what Jesus encountered as He went to the cross. Let me emphasize: in a very, very small way.

In His sufferings, He reached out to us. In His pain, He prayed for us. In His sacrifice, He loved us. In His 33 years of life on earth, He made a way for us to spend eternity with Him. He was showing me how to be light during the dark times. God is light, so isn't afraid of the dark. Consider the following.

It was during the darkness of night that the Israelites crossed the Red Sea.

Daniel faced the lions unscathed during the blackness of night.

The murkiness of night enclosed Jonah in the belly of a fish.

It was pitch black on the Sea of Galilee when Jesus walked on water.

The tomb of Christ was besieged with darkness when He rose.

He is the God of miracles, even in the shadowy times. He asks us to be light to those walking in the blackness of despair.

It was during this season that we came to realize that Jesus never fails. It wasn't that we thought He had or ever would, but knowing it and walking through it are two entirely different things. I had to learn to trust my heavenly Father with each and every step I took in life's desert. My health, my future, my relationships, my past, my emotions, my faith, my character, my calling as a minister, my finances, my worth. My identity.

Kim's entire salary for the year went to pay for my hospital bills. Remember, also, that I'd cancelled several speaking engagements due to multiple surgeries. I look back with complete amazement as I see how God faithfully supplied our every financial need. This verse from the Bible became a reality for us on more than one occasion.

"Once I was young, and now I am old. Yet I have never seen the godly abandoned or their children begging for bread" (Psalm 37:25).

God had not abandoned us!

We would go to our mailbox to discover a gift from someone who had heard of our plight. God was providing through people from across the country—some of whom we had never met. People sent cards, text messages, and phone calls, and prayed fervently for us during this dim season. To say that we were humbled by the generosity of others would be a grave understatement. Trips to the mailbox became tear-filled moments. We were truly blown away in every aspect.

It was now August of 2015. I was still without a job, and because of the ordeal we'd just been through I was unable to seriously search for a position. A few weeks into August we received a phone call for a ministry opportunity. Kim and I believed this would be the turnaround in our lives. Surely this meant we could walk out of the desert and return to the safety of our home.

Step five. (Turn to see if God was still with me.) We met with the pastor of the church, convinced that this was the Lord who had opened the door for us. It had been our prayer all along that God would open or close doors for us. This simply meant we were committed to obey what He opened for us. This was the testing part of Deuteronomy 8:2. We were ready to move and obey, only to have the pastor decide that he wanted to go a different direction. Due to the possibility of moving and taking on a church staff position, we didn't accept any speaking engagements. Now with this position gone, it meant we would go several more months without income. More humbling. More dependence. More testing. In the midst of it all we never missed a payment on a bill and never missed a meal.

Ever watch a movie that you didn't really enjoy but ended up watching it just to see how it would end? This was how I viewed where we were. I certainly didn't like the movie I found myself in as the main character. I watched with intrigue, wanting to know how it would finish, or if it would. What I discovered was that this wasn't a story about me, but rather a story about God and His working in my life. He continued to show Himself to us in ways we hadn't previously experienced.

Why the desert? Yes, to humble and test us. But I believe ultimately to show us who He really is and wants to be in our lives. He was showing me that He loved me and believed in me! Even in the darkest moments of life. He was proving to me that my worth was well beyond five dollars. Just as He was with Peter as he walked on water, God was with me as I walked on sand.

We miss this aspect of a God as we're sitting in our comfortable homes, attending our elaborate churches, comfortable in our secure jobs. It's in the sinister night, walking through the wilderness, that we see the beauty of the God of Light.

In December we interviewed for another position and in January we accepted the invitation. God had opened a door for us and we were ready to boldly march through it. It would mean a move for us but we were just happy to finally be serving the Lord once again. Our start date would be April 15, 2016.

Slowly raise my foot to take the next step. I was straightening things in our home, as the realtor would be coming that afternoon to prepare things for the sale of our home. The phone rang. The call came from a staff member of the church. Seemed a bit strange to get the call but I'd asked for some materials the week before, and thought this must be a follow-up. "Rod, I wanted to let you know that the pastor resigned last night, so we can't offer the position to you. I'm sorry about this."

Please! Someone pinch me! I have to be dreaming. Was this some kind of joke? God, are you serious? This doesn't happen. I set the phone down, sat on the couch, and stared out the window. Ginormous crocodile tears filled my eyes. I'd been here before. I'd become all too familiar with the waterworks that hit the sand beneath me and turned the ground below to mud.

I'm reminded of John 9:6. Jesus spits in the dirt and makes some mud, and then wipes the mud on the man's eyes and the man is able to see. My tears, mixed with the desert sand, became that mud. Jesus was healing my sight. He wanted me to see Him and His working in my life in a clearer fashion. He wanted me to see people the way He sees them. He wanted me to know that I could trust in Him at every moment.

In two years we had lost two ministry positions and two potential ones. Abandonment was knocking at our door. I had to make a decision as to whether or not to answer.

What I haven't mentioned in all of this was that, while all of this is going on, our son and daughter-in-love had just been released from their church in Florida, due to budget issues. And our daughter and son-in-love had just experienced their sixth miscarriage. Our other daughter and son-in-love had just encountered their first miscarriage.

We were doing our best to be good parents and exemplary models of the Christian faith. We questioned our faith. We repented of every sin we knew of, those we didn't know of, and sins we weren't sure if we'd ever committed or even existed—just to be safe. Was the Bible true? Was God real? Maybe we just die one day and that's it. We wondered if we would ever… [fill in the blank]. Too many questions and not enough answers.

Too much sand.

Too dark.

Too many howling creatures.

Too much wilderness.

The journey continues as I write this chapter of our lives and of this book. We live each day by faith, and trust in God as our Provider, Healer, and most of all Savior. We do our best in allowing humility to encompass our lives. The tests continue but our faith continues to grow. God hasn't forsaken us. Rather, He's teaching me how to live abandoned for Him.

Simply put: I may have more steps to take, but I'm not afraid of the dark. He is my Light.

CHAPTER TWELVE

COOL WATCH BRO!

Assemble your life into a platform, not an anchor.

"The Lord is close to the brokenhearted; he rescues those whose spirits are crushed" (Psalm 34:18).

I love sports. As a kid I played just about every sport offered. Not only did I enjoy participating, but if I wasn't engaged in one I was usually watching them on television. It was my way of escaping a dysfunctional home. My addiction included soccer, which wasn't even considered a real sport in America at the time. My introduction to this game occurred during fifth grade, while living in Phoenix. Of course, this was long before the school sanctioned soccer, so I joined a recreational league that met and practiced in the evenings. As a result, practices usually concluded as night settled in on the city park.

A few close friends decided to join me and give it a try, allowing us to carpool to practice since the soccer fields were across the city, approximately a half-hour drive away. Following one particular practice a few of the guys began to make fun of one of our friends. This bantering was quite normal for our group. This night, however, the joking quickly escalated more than was usual.

As the mocking continued, one of the dads pulled into the parking lot. The four of us began to pile in the car when one of my friends turned to the boy being teased and told him they weren't going to give him a ride home. At first we all thought it a joke, but soon it became clear that he wasn't playing. My friend, our friend, was going to be left behind, abandoned at the soccer fields as darkness fell. Perhaps the image is so strong in my mind because it was a convincing reminder of how my life looked. My life was marred by abandonment as darkness was falling, so to speak.

What surprised me, even as a young fifth-grader, was that the dad did nothing to correct this bullying by his son. He simply sat in the driver's seat, hands on the steering wheel, gazing out the windshield. He didn't seem to notice what was taking place—or to care. You somewhat expect 10-year-old boys to act this way, but not dads. The two boys climbed into the vehicle, leaving just enough room for me to sit down in the back seat. But I couldn't do it. There was no way I was going to leave my friend all alone.

No one should be left alone. This night was some sort of a demarcation for me. I would forever be an advocate for those who had to go through life having been left out. Without hesitation I shut the car door, and that father of one of my friends put the car in Drive and left. The two of us stood there watching as the car pulled out of the parking lot, into the busy Phoenix traffic, and eventually out of sight.

Let me remind you that this took place in the 1900s, long before cell phones. Not only would we not be able to phone our parents, but the father who served as the driver that evening couldn't call either of our parents to let them know what happened. I'm not sure he would have anyway. My friend and I sat on one of those parking lot curbs, waiting. It got darker. More people left the park. We grew hungrier. Neither of us was sure how long it would be before one of our parents would come to pick us up.

One of the things you've probably noticed as you've read through my story is that there are certain, specific instances I distinctly remember. These rare flashes shout louder than the numerous other moments in my life. They're etched forever in my memory. It's my hope that you'll be encouraged as you read through the life of an ordinary guy who experienced an upbringing of rejection, abuse, and mayhem, but who turned out all right. (Some may debate whether I turned out right or not!)

I draw your attention to this for one reason.

The Bible is full of stories about real people, individuals who crossed through difficult times. I read stories of people and see their own pain. Their rejection. Abandonment. Questions of self-worth. It's through this unique perspective that I read and apply God's Word. Perhaps this is one reason God included these stories in the first place. I realized that God is more than able to use the pain from our lives in order to help us see more of us. Your Father in heaven is committed to making your past a platform with a message, rather than an anchor that sinks you.

As a result of our disappointments we know the words to speak hope into the lives of others. This is exactly what happened to me on this night, sitting in a parking lot in the middle of Phoenix. I guess there was something in me that wanted my friend to understand he didn't have to walk through life alone. Others can and do care for him.

What he didn't know was that the guy bringing this hope to him was a guy who was struggling to make sense out of his own life. I think it's all right to not have all of life figured out and yet remain a good friend to others.

"May the God of hope fill you with all joy and peace as you trust in him, so that you may overflow with hope by the power of the Holy Spirit" (Romans 15:13).

In 1998, my wife and I took our kids to see the movie *The Prince of Egypt*. It was a cartoon, or "animated film," about the life of Moses. We thought it would be a great film for the kids to see, since it showed a fascinating biblical story in a medium that kids would enjoy. Like most dads who bring their kids to see a children's film, I was focused on if they were enjoying it—while also thinking about other things I could be doing. That is, until the burning bush scene. You know the one. The only time a burning bush talks to anyone. Actually it was God speaking. As He spoke to Moses through the bush, He was also speaking to me as I sat reclining in my seat.

"Take off your sandals," God told Moses. "I've seen how harsh people have been. I don't like how my people are being treated. I want you to do something about it. I want you to get them out of bondage."

I've read this story more times than I can remember, but sitting in the back of the theater that day was like hearing it for the first time. A parade of tears were now marching down my face faster than I could wipe them away. My hands were hiding my face from my family, or anyone else for that matter, so they wouldn't see me crying. I was witnessing how God had been busy cultivating years of preparation in my life, all in order to bring hope and freedom to others.

Prior to Moses having this conversation with God, he'd been abandoned. His mother, Jochebed, had left him in the hands of the Nile River. Not necessarily by choice, but in order to protect him. Nonetheless, he was adopted into a new family. Fast forward 40 years following his adoption. Moses is now living in a desert, spending most of his time alone with sheep. He learns to be a shepherd during these 40 years.

Moses then spends the final 40 years leading the people of Israel out of slavery. He moves from being abandoned by others to being abandoned to God, ultimately abandoned for others. Moses learns this on the backside of a desert while learning how to take care of sheep.

I was born in 1962. It was 2002, 40 years later, that I took on a leadership role to serve 90 churches and youth ministries across the state of Nebraska. This meant that I was responsible for, and intricately involved in, providing some aspect of leadership and training. God took an illegitimate kid and made him into a minister to teenagers from broken homes. Perhaps it's simply coincidence that it was 40 years for Moses and me. But maybe not. Now you understand what I mean when

I say I see things in Scripture through the specific lens of my story. God positions each of us years ahead of time, to fulfill His purpose for others.

Could it be that God took my birth circumstances in 1962, and offered me an opportunity to use them for His greater meaning 40 years later and beyond? I believe so. I'm convinced that He took a boy, born as the result of a bet, with a perceived worldly value of $5, and turned him into a young man with eternal value, worth the death of His Son, to offer hope to others. His death purchased not only my eternal salvation, but an opportunity to speak value into those who struggle to see their own. Perhaps my own abandonment, as difficult as it was, was timed perfectly in order to offer hope to the people I meet. This is my hope. Your story is no different. God desires to take your life and make it into a platform of faith and courage.

Again, I'm in no way suggesting that God plays chess with our lives and moves us around the board against our will. We are free to choose. A child was born, as a result of a blind date. That child was me. I could choose to live in the anchor of my past or lean on my heavenly Father for comfort, healing, and purpose.

Seeing your life in the pages of the Bible is the first step. Rather than simply reading stories about other people, begin to see your name and story in Scripture. If the Bible is just a collection of stories about other individuals, with no application for our lives, then how significant a role does it play in us being able to find God for ourselves?

God not only reveals Himself to us through Scripture, but He tells us stories about us, if we look. Of course, your literal name may never appear in the pages of the Bible. My name only appears as an instrument for a shepherd's use: rod. I do, however, find myself throughout the pages of others, as they trek through life in search of God and His plan.

God fiercely worked in and through the lives of characters. We read how He operated in the lives of Noah, Moses, Ruth, Esther, David,

Daniel, Nehemiah, Peter, Mary, Paul and so many others. Each character in Scripture endured trials, persecution, and heartache, eventually discovering and fulfilling their destiny. We can learn a great deal about ourselves by reading the lives of others and seeing ourselves through their journey.

Consider the life story of Daniel. He finds himself in a lion's den and facing certain death. Can you relate? Have you ever found yourself trapped in a situation with no hope? My guess is you have. But you made it through to the next morning. Your story and Daniel's are similar. No, you didn't have a couple of lions hanging out with you all night. But maybe you did make it through a seemingly impossible situation. Among other reasons, you made it because God is not finished in your life.

"For God is working in you, giving you the desire and the power to do what pleases him" (Philippians 2:13).

I like this verse in Philippians. Notice three things about it. First, God is working in you. Even in the times when you don't believe, He is working in your life. You may find it difficult to believe God is aware of what's going on in your little corner of the world, let alone that He's working on our behalf, but He is. How many times have you or I asked God if He understood what we were going through? How many times have we questioned if God was big enough to handle it? How many times have we asked when God was going to do something to help us? Here's some really good news. Not only is God aware, He's diligently working in and through you and He's big enough to accomplish the task!

Second, God is giving us the desire to do what pleases Him. Isn't this what you want to do as a follower? The more time we spend with Him the more we want to please Him. Finally, God gives us the power to do what pleases Him. Not only does He give us the desire, but He enables us to be able to accomplish it. In the midst of our shortcomings, our pain, and our abandonment, God empowers us to find strength for our lives.

That's outrageous grace at work! You see, our purpose is ultimately found in pleasing Him. We both want and need purpose for our lives, and God beautifully recognizes this need. This goes much further than simply filling a position or having a title or role. Our ultimate destiny is about accepting the power he has to change us, in order that we might please Him.

Often we attribute the acts of God as coincidence or happenstance, when in reality God has been operating with great intentions. We miss the big miracles of God because we're looking for the angels to blow a trumpet and the heavens to part. We discount whether something is a miracle unless it happens instantaneously. The miracles of God not only happen but they come in His timing, as well.

What we fail to see is that God is doing many miracles, when we're completely unaware. What I didn't realize was that God was doing miraculous events for several years, in an illegitimate son. In other words, rather than looking for the miracle, be one! Not only are you a miracle of God, you are a miracle for God.

Grasp the concept that the miraculous isn't meant solely for the recipient. Miracles are always brought to an individual and meant to be shared as a blessing for others! When we consider the burning bush we should understand that the bush wasn't for Moses to get goose bumps or feel good. It wasn't to see a bush not burned up, or to have this amazing conversation with God. The burning bush was never meant to be limited to Moses going home to tell his wife about the incredible experience he had during his day at work.

"So there I was, taking care of the sheep, when all of a sudden, out of nowhere, this bush started burning…"

Moses didn't experience this in order to secure his own television ministry, share on social media, or ask people to send money to receive their own piece of the burning bush. No, this was for the deliverance of

God's people—to deliver hope to those needing it most! God was working in Moses' life for years in order to prepare him for an encounter solely intended to lead people out of bondage. He does this, and wants to do the same in our lives. Imagine if Jesus simply took pleasure in His own resurrection, rather than saw it as what was needed in order to bring hope to others?

God was working in my life, through each puzzle piece I've shared in this book, offering me the opportunity to be part of His story. Just because you don't see the miracle happening doesn't mean that the miracle isn't happening. God is at work in you!

The outpouring of what God was doing wasn't over when I was adopted by a dad, surrendered my life to Christ, or answered the call as a minister. These happenings were just the beginning. The miracle wasn't finished when my multiple surgeries concluded, the doctor visits subsided, and my kidneys got better. The miracle isn't over when we're set free from the bondage of our past. Actually, the miracle is just beginning! If you find yourself still looking for the miracle, let me assure you that it means God is still working for you.

I mentioned earlier that one of my daughters and son-in-love had experienced six miscarriages. But in January of 2017 our second grandson was born to them—a healthy and gorgeous boy. As wonderful a miracle as he is, this isn't the end. It's just the beginning. Yes, we celebrate his birth, but God's purpose in bringing them a child is just beginning. Only God knows what will become of our new little bundle of joy.

One year after my release from another ministry I found myself speaking at a youth convention in Nebraska. I was soon approaching a full year of not having a job—a year with no steady income. Remember that my wife's entire income had gone toward my four surgeries and medical expenses that year.

Following the Friday evening service I was out talking with students in the lobby of the church. This is a regular ritual of mine as I thoroughly enjoy hanging out with teens. Making my way through the various youth groups I happened to stumble upon a group of teens sitting quietly in a circle. Immediately, I knew I would have to do something about this. So I invited myself into their circle ready to have some fun. Moments later I noticed a young man wearing a very nice-looking watch.

Now, I must mention to you that I'm a watch guy. What does this mean? Glad you asked. I love watches. I have a collection of watches, most of them given to me as gifts.

"Wow! That's a cool watch. I love watches and I love your watch. I could never wear a watch like that because it's a cool watch and you're hip and I'm not. I have a watch but not as trendy as yours," I said, attempting to have some fun with the young man.

This continued on for a minute longer when the young man looked at me and said. "If I give you my watch will you wear it?"

Now, I had never met this kid before. I didn't even know his name. It was pure coincidence that I ran into him among more than 600 other students.

"I could never take your watch. Besides, I'm not stylish like you so I couldn't wear it. That watch was meant for cool people like you."

"If I give it to you will you wear it?" he asked a second time.

By now I was totally confused as to what is going on. I looked to the other students in the youth group and asked them if he was being serious. Not that I wanted the watch—I was just curious to know what was happening. They looked at me and told me he was dead serious. By the time I turned back toward the young man, he had removed his watch and was handing it to me.

To most this may appear as nothing more than some old guy getting a cool watch from a young man. But as I mentioned before, I'm a watch guy. What's utterly amazing is that God knows I'm a watch guy. That November night in Nebraska, God reminded me that He hadn't forgotten me. The timepiece was a small way to convey to me that He was still working. Most wouldn't see the watch as a miracle, but I did. In some way it was my burning bush. It was a reminder that He loved me.

As I stated earlier, miracles are just the beginning. I receive more compliments on that watch than all my other watches combined. This allows me to share the story of God's timeless love.

God's subtle reminders in our lives are part of a life designed with and for purpose. Abraham and Sarah having a miracle child at their old age was the beginning. Boaz and Ruth miraculously meeting was the launch of the lineage of King David, eventually leading to the birth of Christ. David killing Goliath was the start of his legacy. Nehemiah miraculously building a broken-down wall was an introduction. Joseph and Mary's baby was a foreword to the finality of sin's power. Jesus' miracle on the cross was the activation of new life for billions and billions of people. There are many more stories I could mention from the Bible. Again, this is why you and I must see ourselves in its pages. Your name is in it!

Allow me to remind us of a verse quoted earlier in the book.

"The Lord directs the steps of the godly. He delights in every detail of their lives" (Psalm 37:23).

God not only knows your details, but delights in every detail of your life.

Each and every one.

Including watches

CHAPTER THIRTEEN

DELAYED DESTINY

Your destiny matters far more than your history.

"The Lord is close to the brokenhearted; he rescues those whose spirits are crushed" (Psalm 34:18).

"And those who know your name put their trust in you, for you, O Lord, have not forsaken those who seek you" (Psalm 9:10).

There are moments in our lives when we feel as if God is silent, when in reality He's clearly speaking to us. We just fail to hear or recognize His voice. God continually speaks to us. His Word forever remains at our disposal. Opening His Word we hear Him speaking to us and revealing to us our ultimate destiny. It's in the midst of this unleashed potential that we often encounter delays. Thus one more reason for securing time in and with God's Word.

It's difficult to pinpoint the moment I collided with my delayed destiny. Perhaps it wasn't one specific moment but rather a process of events that slowly trickled into my life. Jesus placed spiritual markers in my path that led to His greater objective. Think of them as a mile marker on the interstate. Just as a mile marker indicates your location, a spiritual marker determines your position, how far you've come in your journey and whether or not you're heading in the right direction.

One significant indicator Jesus set before me occurred in the winter of 1996. I had joined the pastoral staff of a good church in Nebraska, but less than two years later I found myself on a plane flying to Springfield, Missouri, to interview for a youth pastor position at a large church.

As I sat in the window seat peering through the small glass opening I couldn't help but notice the vast farmland surrounding the airport. As the small jet lowered its landing gear I saw what I believed to be our new home and ministry location. The wheels screeched as they hit the runway, and I heard someone speak to me. No one was sitting in the aisle seat next to me, so I could only conclude that the Lord speaking. Though it wasn't an audible voice, it was as close to one as I've ever heard. So much so that I thought one of the passengers behind me might have said something.

"Welcome home," the voice said.

Welcome home?

I'd never been to Springfield. If it was God speaking to me, He had clearly overlooked this one fact. One thing I've learned over the years is that God is never wrong. This one fact strongly indicates that I haven't caught up with His plan.

Arriving at my hotel I phoned my wife to tell her the short conversation I had just had with God. Actually, it wasn't much of a conversation. He had just spoken two words to me. That was it. No explanation. No details. No answers.

"I think we're moving to Missouri," I said to my wife.

Silence.

We had just moved to Nebraska and I was now presenting the idea that we would be relocating once again. Not exactly what my wife wanted to hear. Not what she needed to hear. She needed to establish roots. We had four kids, and the last thing she wanted was to uproot our family once again after such a short time in our current assignment. She knew I was unhappy with the present situation but the thought of packing boxes and loading a truck; selling a home; buying a new one; finding new schools, new doctors, new friends; and saying goodbye to people we had forged relationships with was a bit unnerving.

It wasn't that big a deal for me. I had grown up in an environment where moving was the norm. Kim, on the other hand, had lived in the same home, in the same small town, from birth through college. As a matter of fact, her parents had lived in the same home for 60 years before going to assisted living. It's funny how God brings together people from such diverse backgrounds to do life together. The two-becoming-one plan of God means both parties must be willing to make necessary sacrifices. You can't fit two into one, so both need to give up a bit of themselves in order to fit. Without a doubt, God was going to shape both of us in this process.

"Trust in the Lord with all your heart; do not depend on your own understanding. Seek his will in all you do, and he will show you which path to take" (Proverbs 3:5-6).

God has a perfect plan for us. Each step along the way I did my best to walk in His great scheme with boldness—living my life with complete abandonment to His will. My wife and I definitely desired to set our lives in the center of abandonment. First, God had to grab our undivided attention. Kim needed to learn to trust God with each move, physical and spiritual, and I needed to learn to be content in each and every situation He placed us. It's not always an issue of who is right; rather, it's allowing God to work through us and bring us to a peaceful dependence on Him.

Over the next couple of days I met with the lead pastor of the church and a few staff members, and toured the massive facility. We enjoyed a few meals together, discussing what the ministry assignment would entail and what the pastor was looking for in a youth pastor. I left fairly confident that I would be offered the position and would need to have some serious discussions with Kim over whether we felt God was moving us from Nebraska to Missouri. I couldn't get away from the fact that I had heard God speak "Welcome home" to me as I flew into Springfield.

I call it delayed destiny. God has a specific plan and unique purpose for your life but the timing of His plan is delayed. There are times when He prophetically speaks to us His future intent in order to prepare our hearts for His purposes. Unfortunately, many (including myself) become so entrenched in the purpose that we overlook the timing. This was the oversight I had done.

A few days following my return to Nebraska the pastor called me to tell me that he had decided to move in a different direction. He was going to hire someone else to fill the role. I thanked him for the opportunity and hung up the phone. I sat at my desk somewhat bewildered.

Had I missed God?

Looking back I now realize I hadn't missed God—just His timing. Like several other examples in the Bible, God had given me a dream that wasn't to be fulfilled for several years to come. Ten years, to be exact. This may sound like a lot of time but Joseph had to wait approximately 22 years to see his dream come about. King David waited about 15 years from the time he was anointed by Samuel until the time he took the throne. Abraham and Sarah waited 13 years for the promise of a son who would fulfill God's purpose for their lives. Of course, let's not forget, Moses, Ruth, Daniel, Esther, Paul, Elisha, and Jacob. Even Jesus found Himself waiting until the appointed time to fulfill His ultimate destiny.

Don't rush God's timing...rest in it. There's a rhythm to His movement. There's as much meaning in God's timing as there is in God's destiny for your life.

"This vision is for a future time. It describes the end, and it will be fulfilled. If it seems slow in coming, wait patiently, for it will surely take place. It will not be delayed" (Habakkuk 2:3).

What fascinates me about the purposes of God is that the dream He gives us is always greater than we initially perceived. That is, if we wait for the vision to come about at the right time. So it is that during the maturing we must learn to rest in God and trust Him with the process. During seasons of waiting we're to boldly seek Him and dedicate ourselves to grow in relationship with Him. This is the reason God breathes destiny into our lives in the first place. It's the period of time between that moment we realize we're in need of healing, the revelation of the vision, and the fulfillment of it that He grooms us. God's perfect timing is all part of the process.

Had I rushed to Springfield in 1996, I would have completely missed out on the greater dream God had for my life. God still had transforming work He needed to do in my life. Never mistake a "not yet" from God as a "no" from God. It's during the "not yet" of life that God wants us to find rest in Him and learn of Him. It's a delayed destiny. All that God had been doing in my life up to this point was part of His design, shaping me in this moment. But He still had 10 years of transformational training before I would be ready to take the next step.

In the spring of 2005, almost 10 years after my plane ride and God speaking "Welcome home" to me, we found ourselves unexpectedly moving to Springfield, Missouri! Through a series of events that I could not have orchestrated in my wildest imagination, God opened doors for us to serve as a national director of youth ministries for our denomination. Ten years earlier I would have been a youth pastor in a local church. That would have been a tremendous privilege in and of itself, but God had another idea in mind. A delayed one. Now I saw how God had us wait for the exact moment in order to step into His greater scheme for our lives.

I stumbled across this on social media, and I believe it may capture the essence of the journey you find yourself on.

"Sometimes you think you're being buried, when you're really being planted. God is using this season to grow you."

Why does God plant us deep within the soil—10 years deep, sometimes? So that our lives bring forth greater fruit when we finally peek through the soil. The deeper He plants us the higher He wants to take us. What I realized later was that God used my years in Nebraska to groom me, mold me, shape me, transform me, humble me, prepare me, and teach me. All for the purpose of stepping boldly into His calling, to continue my journey of complete abandonment to Him! How different my life would be if it was to be one solely about survival. Success in life isn't measured by survival. Rather, God intends to take us from a state of being abandoned by others to living a life of abandonment for others.

Do you see how far God has brought you? When I consider this in my own life I realize that I once thought I would be unable to even enter the sanctuary. You remember the verse in Deuteronomy?

"If a person is illegitimate by birth, neither he nor his descendants for ten generations may be admitted to the assembly of the Lord" (Deuteronomy 23:2). Yet from May 2005 until December of 2013, God's fate placed me in a key role in youth ministry at a national level. I entered countless sanctuaries all over the world during this time. My life was no longer a story about me, but it was about who God is and what He is capable of doing in a surrendered life. God is able to see you through each aspect of His call for your life. It's really a matter of us being willing to travel through the process.

As I write this, I now find myself in a completely new season of life. For the past 28 years I served in ministry working with a group of people. For the past couple of years the Lord has had me on a unique journey, being on my own, speaking, writing, coaching, and consulting, all to serve the Church. I've established a non-profit ministry to continue in what we believe the next step for our lives is. Once again, not in my wildest imagination could I have seen myself doing this. God has intentionally arranged each step of our journey. He desires to do the same for you. Rest in His call and timing for your life. He has dreams for you that you could not possibly see at this point in your life and every day you are one step closer.

Fast forward 10 years following our move to Springfield. It's now been about 20 years from hearing God speak to me just above the runway. Attending my home church as I had done on many Sundays, the pastor unveiled a new church wide theme. The new theme?

Welcome Home!

Some 20 years after hearing those two words on a flight from Omaha to Springfield, those two simple words appear on the giant screens in the church auditorium. Coincidently, these two words appeared at a time when we needed them the most. We found ourselves entering a new chapter in our lives. We were home as we found ourselves on our own in ministry. It was God's gentle and gigantic reminder. Much like every call God gives us, we don't know how long we will be here, but God confirmed His plan and that we were exactly where we belonged.

God has given you a dream. A destiny. He hasn't forgotten it or you. The delay is a result of His working in your life, all in preparation for next steps. He still has purpose for your life. He knows the details of His plan and your life and is tirelessly working to bring it about in your life. You may feel He's forgotten all about you. But you're in a period of rest. Don't rush it. Rest. You may feel buried. Don't poke your head above the ground just yet. Let Him continue to mature you for the next season. Now is the time to kneel at the altar of His presence and commune with Him.

I believe God has revealed His plan to you for the next season. Perhaps you thought it was for now, when in reality it's yet to come. This is a time of refreshing. This is a time of renewing relationships and restoration of your soul. You are being prepared for the dream He has placed in your heart. You remember that dream? It may have been 10 years or 20 years ago, but it remains. God has not forgotten.

I can imagine what some of you may be thinking at this point. You may believe you're too old for God to do anything new in your life. This is exactly what Abraham and Sarah thought when the Lord spoke to them about their own new season. God is always moving us toward a new season, no matter what the age. It's when we stop moving toward Him and what He has for our lives that we stop growing. Just as Abraham and Sarah had a child at their old age, God is birthing something new in your life. He wants you pregnant! Relax…not that kind of pregnant—or maybe!

You may feel you're too young. Consider Mary. She was a young teen and yet gave birth to the Son of God, Jesus. God is not only birthing something new in your life, He is birthing something meant to bring life to others.

You may believe the sin you've committed is too big for God to forgive. You've lost hope that God could make something wonderful from your life. Tell that to King David. He committed adultery and then murder. What about the deceiver, Jacob? Let's not forget Moses, who murdered, or Paul, who had Christians killed. Rahab was a prostitute, and Peter, one of Jesus' closest friends and disciples, denied Jesus three times. Each life is a reminder that God uses ordinary people with flaws. Your Father in heaven has not forgotten you!

Remember the road markers I spoke of earlier? Along the highways of our journey, God sends us small markers to show us we are on the right path. If you're not looking for them, you miss them. It's amazing how many markers one can pass before noticing one. As you travel down the interstate these markers appear every tenth of a mile, a constant reminder of how far you've travelled and how much farther you have to go to reach your destination. Our spiritual markers appear during our spiritual voyage. Unlike the interstate markers, however, these spiritual roadside markers don't seem to have the same consistency or frequency of the ones we cruise by in our vehicles. No, our spiritual markers seem to arrive at times we least expect, and because of this they may go completely unnoticed. Such was the case for me in February of 2015.

I had lost my second ministry position in a year and was feeling lost, forsaken, and completely abandoned by God. Wait! Isn't this just after seeing that ginormous screen-shot of "Welcome Home"? Yes it is. I guess there are moments in my life when I allow my feelings to override my faith. Losing another ministry position was not what I signed up for, to say the least. I had it in my mind that following Jesus meant a life free from difficulties. You know this life I speak of? The kind of life that includes having a superior-paying job, excellent health, a stress-free home life, a faithful spouse, loyal friends, dependable transportation—a worry-free, anxiety-exempt, life. But when I do a quick search of the Scriptures I find that Jesus never promised this to us. Rather, in the midst of the storms of life, He said He would be with us and would calm the storms.

Just a few weeks after what seemed to be my second ministry failure, I found myself in Arizona for a speaking engagement that had been on the books for several months. The pastor graciously allowed me to speak on the originally scheduled Sunday though I would no longer be communicating on behalf of the ministry as we had originally scheduled. The trip to Arizona not only meant some much-needed income for us, but also meant I would be able to spend a few days with my son-in-love and daughter, who lived just a few hours from the church I would be ministering.

One evening my daughter, Bethany, son-in-love, Griffin, and I found ourselves sitting in the living room of their home when Griffin handed me a wrapped box.

"Happy early birthday," he said as he handed me the box. "I know your birthday isn't for several weeks, but I wanted to give this to you rather than mail it."

To say I was caught completely by surprise would be a gross understatement. I thanked him for the gift and proceeded to open it. Removing the wrapping paper I saw a black case.

Let me mention that in addition to being a watch guy, I'm also a pen guy. Specifically, I like Mont Blanc pens. I know, right? But if you're going to like pens you might as well like the expensive ones! Anytime I'm traveling and see a Mont Blanc store I will stop in just to write with a few of the pens and drool over them.

I opened the pen box. Tears clouded my eyes. There was a Mont Blanc pen, beautifully resting in the case! But it was much more than a pen that I would never be able to afford. It was a spiritual marker in my journey, much like the watch I had received earlier. Remember, you have to look for these or they pass right by. God was prompting me that He was aware of the road I was traveling on and wanted me to know that the road was clearly marked out for me.

Coincidence you say? I couldn't disagree more. There's always a backstory with God when He has you pass by a marker. Allow me to tell you this one. As I mentioned in a previous chapter, Griffin's dad had passed away about 10 years prior to this. What I didn't know was that Griffin's dad, Mark, was also a Mont Blanc pen guy.

Following Mark's death his things were packed in boxes and stored away. It wasn't until years later that Griffin's mom began giving the boxes to her boys. As Griffin opened one of the boxes he discovered his father's Mont Blanc pen. He decided to give his dad's pen to me. Once again, God had taken a somewhat casual moment and turned it into a gracious, gentle, gigantic reminder that He was with me. Think about it. It wasn't until years after Mark's passing that the box was opened, and it happened to be at the exact moment of my visit, just after losing my second ministry position in a year. And it was a Mont Blanc pen. God's timing is perfect. It's up to us to recognize it.

In our attempt to see the big miracles of God we often miss the little moments with God.

"When I look at the night sky and see the work of your fingers—the moon and the stars you set in place—what are mere mortals that you should think about them, human beings that you should care for them?" (Psalm 8:3-4).

Mere man is so small compared to the vastness of the universe and all that God created, and yet He chooses to keep us near Him in thought and deed. When I consider my life began as a result of a five-dollar bet, I'm tempted to think that my life is somewhat insignificant. But then I'm amazed that the God of the universe, of all creation, thought about me in a living room in Phoenix by handing me a pen. This is outrageous grace! He deeply cares, down to the smallest detail. I simply can't afford to place my identity in a five-dollar bill. I have to place it in what the Creator of the universe did for me! He cares for me...and He cares for you!

These tender reminders of a pen and a watch speak to me of a God who genuinely thinks and acts on every detail of my life. I'm astounded that my value isn't determined by what I think of myself or the opinions of others, but rather what God did for me in sending His Son, Jesus. The death of God's only Son expresses the beautiful value God places on my life. Not only did His death show us the miraculous—purchasing our eternal salvation, but the moment of His death spoke of the value He places on our lives and His purpose for us. The Old Testament individual, Joseph learned the purpose of his delayed destiny found in verse 20 of Genesis 50.

"You intended to harm me, but God intended it all for good. He brought me to this position so I could save the lives of many people."

As I mentioned before, Joseph experienced total abandonment by his family, was sold into slavery, faced wrongful accusation involving the raping of a woman, was thrown into a brutal prison, and completely forgotten by all. Out of all of this he could have, and had every right to, become extremely bitter, blaming family and friends for the years he spent abandoned in isolation and rejection. Instead Joseph stayed the course, remaining faithful in his relationship with God, completely abandoned to Him and His purposes.

Most people in our world have endured abandonment, undergone countless struggles in life, and faced extreme difficulty finding clarity and meaning. Keep in mind that God designed us to not only have divine objectives but to reach the destiny He's outlined for our lives. This is just one reason the enemy of our souls does all he can to isolate us through abandonment, and convince us we're of little or no value. Putting into question our worth diminishes our belief that we can accomplish what God has for our lives. We end up going through life with feelings of inadequacy, fears of failing, and on a desperate search to belong.

This is why Genesis 50:20 should completely capture our attention. God makes good in our lives, on what the enemy meant for harm! Our abandonment came at great cost to God the Father. The enemy intended to harm us and leave us abandoned through life, but God is more than capable to use it for His good—to save the lives of many people. Your purpose remains regardless of how you arrived or whether or not you feel worthy enough to fulfill that purpose. Could it be that God is working in your delayed destiny to bring hope and life to others?

I grew up feeling abandoned by family and others, but through Christ I've come to a place in my life where I'm now abandoned to Christ! We haven't been called by God to live a life abandoned to fear, doubt, rejection, or pain. We've been chosen and positioned to live a life abandoned to God and for God and the destiny He has. This hope gives me a true sense of usefulness! I heard one person say, "Your destiny matters far more than your history."

All my life I've wanted a home. The invitation to come home was given to me on an airplane. Over the next 10 years my Father in heaven was preparing my heart for a homecoming. You see, coming to Springfield was a sign of God's continuing healing and restoration in my life.

God has a homecoming for you, as well. He's been preparing yours for months, or even years. Don't delay. It's in this moment that He longs to restore your soul, renew your relationships, and breathe purpose into your life.

He whispers to you.

Welcome Home!

CHAPTER FOURTEEN

TATTOOED

"You were born with the ability to change someone's life. Don't ever waste it." –Anonymous

I lived in California during junior high. It was during this period of my life that two events forever shaped my calling, although I didn't realize it at the time.

Margo was a beautiful, blonde junior-high classmate of mine. I think just about every boy in my school had a crush on her, including me. As it turned out one of my good friends asked her to go steady. This meant there would be an exchanging of rings and an "off limits" to other individuals. This act by my friend brought much heartache to many a young man in my school. The two of them dated for a good portion of the school year before breaking up with each other.

Once a couple was going steady it meant that the guy would walk the girl to each of her classes. They would, of course, hold hands the entire way. Upon arrival at the next class, they would stand outside the classroom, waiting for all the other students to pass by, before kissing each other. It was not some insignificant kiss, either. I know this, as I witnessed many of them taking place during my junior high years. This ritual took place throughout each passing period, each day of the week.

After what seemed to be an eternity of dating, the two of them broke up, leaving Margo available. Several of my friends then began to inform me of Margo's love for me and that she wanted me to ask her to go steady. I should at this point mention that I was a pretty shy individual, but the pressure I felt from others eventually got to me.

Every morning students were required to wait in the gym prior to the first bell announcing our first class of the day. So it was that one particular morning the two of us found ourselves standing directly in front of one another. I must admit that her innocence and beauty weakened my knees, followed by six words exiting my mouth.

"Will you go steady with me?" I asked.

"Yes," she said.

The bell rang, announcing our first class and my first attempt to lock lips with her. I hadn't had much practice at all during my 13 years on earth. We walked to her class without holding hands. This was a clear violation of the junior-high, going-steady Code of Conduct. I can't imagine what she was thinking after spending several months of hand-holding with my friend.

Why isn't he holding my hand?

We arrived at the kissing fields when I turned to her and said, "So, I'll see you later." Then I turned and ran to my first class. No kiss, no hand-holding, no more going steady. I'd had enough romance, so I avoided her the rest of the day. Later that day she ran up to me and asked what was going on. I told her that I wanted to break up with her. This may go down as the shortest dating phase in history.

There is one other strong memory I have from that same school year. Once every year a student was chosen to be the teacher in each class. In seventh grade I was voted to be the science teacher. A different student would be chosen for math, history, and so on. Additionally, the students with the highest votes served as principal, vice principal, and boys and girls counselors. By virtue of receiving enough votes, during eighth grade I was voted the boys counselor. This meant I spent the entire day in the office of Mr. Mooney, the boys counselor.

We spent the morning sitting in his office appearing to look like we were doing something extremely important. Truth be told, we really just sat there discussing my interests. That is, until lunch.

"I'm heading to lunch and then I'll be running some errands. The errands will take most of the afternoon, so I won't be back today," Mr. Mooney stated. "You're in charge now." With that, he left for the day. I sat back in his large, leather chair prepared for an afternoon of relaxation.

What I hadn't yet realized was that I was about to come face to face with one of those life-shaping encounters. The entire run-in would only take a few moments but it would tattoo me, leaving a permanent impression on my soul and future. God was busy preparing me for a purpose far greater than me. I was being prepared to live abandoned. As I write each chapter I'm fascinated by the fact that God was always working in and through me. He never gave up on me.

Following lunch I began issuing hall passes to my buddies. This allowed them to get out of class, as they would now have to report to the boys counselor: yours truly. We would spend the class period drinking soda, eating candy, and talking about all the things that eighth-grade boys talk about. At the end of the counseling session (class period) I would write my friends a pass that allowed them back into their class before the bell rang. I also issued a pass for the next period, enabling them to once again come to my office to receive much-needed help for the many issues facing 13-year-old boys. After all, I was the boys counselor. It was my sworn duty. This went on throughout the remainder of the afternoon.

I had just sent my friends back to their class, issuing them a hall pass for the final period of the day. In between each subject was a five-minute passing period, followed by another five minutes for teachers to record attendance, before my friends could join me.

As students made their way to their last lesson, in walked Cindy. There were several things wrong with this scenario, least of which was that a girl had just walked into the boys counselor's office. What made this even more troubling for me was that Cindy was one of those individuals who had experienced more pain and rejection in junior high than most people undergo in their lifetime. Cindy had many issues that plagued her life, which led to constant, and at times severe, teasing by classmates. She was unattractive, had a severe speech impediment, and mental and physical challenges. This combination brought about constant verbal abuse from just about every junior-high student, including me. I sat in my large, leather chair, staring at a young girl who endured the pain of abandonment.

Sitting in front of me and across Mr. Mooney's desk sat my defined purpose. Although I didn't realize it at that moment, looking back I realize how God had orchestrated this one-in-a-million chance encounter. God was preparing an abandoned young boy to now live a life completely abandoned, in order to bring hope to those who had been abandoned.

With tears streaming down her face she told me how everyone made fun of her, called her names, would physically push her—the list of hurts continued to pour from her broken heart. I sat speechless. The chances that I would have just enough votes for this office, or that Mr. Mooney would leave for the day and leave me sitting in his office alone, or that Cindy would walk into the boy's counselor office was more than happenchance. What was I to do? I was just a 13-year-old boy. That one confrontation made such an impact on my young life that I did my best to never make fun of anyone from that day forward.

Although I didn't fully recognize it at the time, this was a definite turning point in my life. I had encountered two girls, extremely opposite from one another, during my eighth-grade year. Margo was beautiful and popular. Cindy fell on the other end of the spectrum. God used these to introduce me to myself.

He was revealing not just His heart, but my heart as well. How had all my past experiences shaped who I was and who I would become in life? I'm thoroughly convinced God does the same for each of us. He uses seemingly innocent moments in our life to pull the scales from our eyes so we can see our purpose in life.

I chose Cindy. Not to date. She didn't even know she was chosen. I chose who she represented in life. She represented the one who had been abandoned. And those who had gone through life experiencing rejection. People who feel life has given up on them. These are the ones I choose to pursue, hold hands with, and walk with on life's journey. As I look back upon my life I guess I've always chosen the Cindy's of the world.

Choosing to live abandoned for the One who abandoned Himself for me!

"For we are God's masterpiece. He has created us anew in Christ Jesus, so we can do the good things he planned for us long ago" (Ephesians 2:10).

Long before my illegitimate birth, God had set in motion a plan for my life. I wasn't a mistake, accident, or error. I was His masterpiece, created for the purpose of doing good things. Good things that He had planned for us long ago. The same holds true for your life. Your Father in heaven has perfectly designed a plan aimed to bring fulfillment to your life and you bring life to others.

We had gathered in my daughter's room for a family game night in February of 2000. Within moments of the first move our phone rang. I jumped up to answer a phone call that would once again propel my life forward into greater discovery.

"Gary's been in an accident. Can you watch our dog? I'm going to drive to Kearney, Nebraska, to meet him," was the panicked voice on the other end. "He can't feel his legs." It was Gary's wife, Laurie.

The car that Gary and his son were in had rolled several times down the intestate, finally resting in the snow-covered grass that separated west- and east-bound traffic along I-80. The two of them were now in the ambulance that would take them to the hospital. Realizing that Laurie and her daughter were in no condition to make the three-hour drive, I volunteered to drive them.

Life is a series of unexpected twists and turns, with each one leaving us careening down our own road of destiny. With each occurrence we're awakened to the idea that God carefully places us with tremendous intentionality. It was no accident that God had done so in my life that night. For me it became a season that would once again test my character, compassion, and competence.

Over the next couple of days and nights I waited with Gary and Laurie's family and friends for what would be a devastating diagnosis. Gary would undergo surgery, leaving him a quadriplegic. He would spend the following couple of months in a rehabilitation hospital to receive the necessary care and therapy. Additionally, this would mean that I, along with the other pastors on staff would spend one or two nights a week staying with him so Laurie could get much-needed rest.

As you can imagine, the Sunday following the accident was immensely emotional. As the senior associate pastor of our 1,000-member church I was called upon to deliver the news and help bring support to the congregation. I stood on the platform staring at the people. They were now without their shepherd, without any idea of how long it would be. Tears were shed, and questions of why filled the auditorium.

I delivered the news to the people in the same sanctuary where I had spent many mornings in prayer. It would be the area where God changed my name. This was the place I had cried out to God following the dismissal of one of our key leaders. It was here I questioned whether I would even be allowed to enter the sanctuary due to my illegitimate birth.

Every bit of character, compassion, and competency was tested during what would end up being approximately a seven-month period. I was called upon to speak most of the Sundays during this time and, as you can imagine, take on additional responsibilities. I can't say enough good things about the other staff members and individuals who made up the church. Without a doubt their love and support made this journey a much easier one.

How does one lead without becoming the leader? No one teaches this in school. I wasn't the chief shepherd of the church, nor would I become it. But I was called upon to hold the hands of the church as we walked. All of this during a very rough stretch of road.

God had positioned me not simply to test me but also because He trusted me. He saw something in me that I didn't see in myself. He does this in our lives. You may not see it, but He places you in crucial moments in order for you to see yourself as He sees you. He was moving me beyond a life of being abandoned to one of abandonment for His cause. In this instant, God needed a shepherd who would not seek his own promotion, but instead would help others who now felt abandoned. Lest you think I handled all of this perfectly, allow me to put your mind at ease. Remember, God trusted me but He remained steadfast in testing me as well. Why? Because He knew I would need to grow from this experience in order to be prepared for the next one, and the next one, and the one after that.

You may recall the storm Peter and the other disciples found themselves in. Out of nowhere, Jesus appears, walking on the water! In that moment of chaos, and a miraculous display of power over nature, Peter asks to walk on water with Jesus. Jesus agrees. Peter steps out of the boat, takes a few steps, and begins to sink. The only part of the story that feels different than mine is that Peter asked to walk on water.

I didn't. I knew I wouldn't be able to walk on the water. Rather, Jesus asks us to walk out to Him. In the torrential rains, hammering waves, and midnight skies Jesus bids us to step out. He is calling you out of the boat even now.

Take that first step. Yes, it's a scary step. The first one usually is.

We've seen the paintings of Peter sinking in the sea as God reaches out to him. God is busily sketching your life's masterpiece. Our work of art is one that takes time to create in order that we can live a life abandoned for Him. God continually calls us into deeper waters to teach us to rely on Him. Peter had faith in Jesus or he wouldn't have asked to get out of the boat. I believe Jesus was showing Peter that He had faith in Peter! He wanted Peter to no longer doubt in his own heart that God was with him. He is with you as you walk on top of the water, and as you and I sink in a sea of doubt. To God's glory, and Gary and Laurie's perseverance and strength, the two of them continue to pastor the church as I write this chapter some 18 years later.

Being an illegitimate, abandoned child of the sixties left me doubting my ability to walk on top of life's deep waters. Questioning my worth and value only served to hamper the full use of my gifts. I spent much of my life just hoping to make it through this thing called life. I simply wanted to survive. Thankfully, we serve a God who spends time with us, preparing us for new seasons and greater reasons. He meticulously works through our past, our pain, and the bitter feelings of rejection in order to bring us to a place of healing.

Living in the misfortune of our past leads us to look back, questioning God and ourselves. Sadly, too many people spend the end of their lives filled with regret rather than the joy of a life well spent. The reward that comes from living an abandoned life for the One who gave His life for us!

Perhaps your life, like mine, has been marred by abandonment. You found yourself replaying the awful moments you've experienced, as you've turned the pages of this book. The moment your dad left you. The instant your parents told you they no longer wanted you. That minute your spouse said they found another. That instance you were placed in foster care or asked your foster parents who your real parents were and why they had left you. Seeing your parent embrace another person. The abuse you suffered. The alcoholism that destroyed your home. The death of a loved one that came much too early. The day your closest friend turned their back on you, when you most needed them. The day...

You wonder if there's still time to make a difference. Is it too late? You question if you still have value or ever had value at all. You're uncertain about your worth to others. Let me assure you, it's never too late! The fact that you're still reading this book indicates that not only do you desire to make a difference but that your mission isn't over.

You understand what it means to be abandoned. You know what it's like to be left out. You understand the feelings of being deserted. You know the feeling of walking through deep, dark valleys. Your life is filled with perspective and insights that few others have. You've been on the backside of the desert waiting to be placed by God—to bring freedom, hope, love, and healing to others. You've been gossiped about, lied to, and manipulated to the point that you can read people and situations with utter clarity. You've experienced sickness and loss. Why? Could it be that the trials and sufferings we face are not without purpose?

Recall King David's words from the 23 Psalm. "Even when I walk through the darkest valley..." His trials served to help him keep his eyes on his King. The misfortunes he faced brought him to a place of utter dependence. The depths of each valley he faced led him to a Father in heaven who remained faithfully at David's side.

Some are architects of their own troubles and shame. They've built fences from offenses. They've erected barricades out of bitterness. They've twisted the lies from their past to form pillars of pain. A million mistakes have been made. Can I bring a word of hope and encouragement to you? Whether you brought on the pain yourself or whether others constructed it, God is more than willing and completely able to reposition you to live utterly abandoned for Him. The enemy of your soul is bent on keeping your eyes focused on your past. He does this so you avoid seeing what God has for you in the days ahead.

Joy awaits!

Your purpose is found on the paths you're on!

I can no longer go through life trying to make sense of my own abandonment or questioning my own worth. I was bought with a price, the price of God's only Son. My purchase price cost the life of God's Son and has eternal value. I have worth, purpose, and legacy in the Kingdom of God. This is my identity, not what happened on a summer evening in California in 1961. Now is the time to bring assurance to people who desperately need to know they're both wanted and desperately loved.

There are too many hurting and homeless, hungry and hopeless. There are those who've been abandoned and abused; are addicted and afraid; are lost and lonely; and are broken, bitter, or barren. Too many are in pain, purposeless, persecuted, thirsty, or tired. People are suffering and scared, depressed, discouraged, or destitute. People need a Savior. People need someone who understands what it's like to be abandoned so they can live abandoned.

Recall in Matthew 27:46 Jesus calls out, "My God, my God, why have you abandoned me?" Just after Jesus speaks these words to His Father, He shouts the following words found in Luke 23:46.

"Father, I entrust my spirit into your hands!" These were the final words Jesus spoke before He breathed His final breath on the cross.

It was at this moment of feeling the pain of sin and abandonment that Jesus committed His life into the hands of His Father. Jesus totally trusted God, His Father, with His life and future. Jesus literally put His life into the hands of His Father. We do the same as we surrender our lives to God. As we completely trust our lives our true Father, we are believing that God will resurrect the hopes, renew our vision, and restore the dreams placed deep inside of us long ago. We now choose to live with complete abandonment toward God and the purposes He has for us. We give ourselves to the hope within us.

Our vision begins to increase as we see the needs of the world differently than we had in the past. Our dreams set aside for His. We no longer view life being about ourselves; we view life as being about helping others in the midst of their pain. We're now committed to securing a place of victory for others.

God has called us to live bold, courageous lives for Him. We've been empowered to display a fierce love, extreme joy, and intense generosity toward people—abandoned for Him. Finding our life story within the pages of the Bible is where it begins for each of us.

Without a doubt one of the greatest privileges I've had was taking students, parents, and youth leaders to Israel to walk where Jesus walked. I was able to lead three trips, taking each of my two boys, Michael and Christopher, on a trip during their senior year in high school.

Each outing included approximately 10 days of sightseeing, ministry moments, baptisms in the Jordan River, visits to Masada, floating on the Dead Sea, walking the streets of Jerusalem, eating fish from the Sea of Galilee, riding camels, and shopping. Definitely something I will both remember and cherish for the rest of my life.

Prior to the trip with each of my boys, I asked about a dozen men I highly respected to write a letter to my boys. Each of these men were fathers themselves and understood the value of raising young men. These letters challenged my sons, encouraged them, and spoke life into them from many fathers. After gathering their letters I placed them in a folder and handed them the letters while in Israel. So many letters had been both written and delivered over thousands of years in Israel. We refer to them as the books of the Old and New Testament. My letters do not compare in the least with the letters of the Bible, but my prayer is that my boys would always remember the significance of receiving them in Israel. These letters from myself and other spiritual fathers were one more attempt to change the course of history for my family.

People would often ask me after returning to the states what was the one aspect of the trip that I most enjoyed. Without hesitation, I'd say our boat ride on the Sea of Galilee. I suppose one reason for this was the fact that most of the ministry of Jesus took place near or on the Sea of Galilee.

The boat ride always took place at night, making it all the more memorable. As night fell over the lake (the Sea of Galilee is a lake and not a sea), I would lean over the rail of the small tour boat, imagining myself as a disciple traveling with Jesus. Each of the three rides were moments of quiet reflection and intimacy as worship music was being played over the speakers of the boat. I'm not positive about this but I would bet that the disciples sang together many a night as they skimmed across the lake.

A piece of trivia that caught my attention while traveling the land of Israel was the vast difference between the Sea of Galilee and the Dead Sea. The two bodies of water are separated by 65 miles, connected by the Jordan River. As I previously mentioned we spent considerable time at both locations. The Sea of Galilee remains a commercial fishing industry just as it did in the days of Jesus and the disciples. You may recall that Jesus called many of His disciples while they were finishing a fishing expedition.

The Dead Sea, on the other hand, cannot sustain life. It is so salty that nothing is able to live in it. One of our outings included a trip to the Dead Sea to go swimming. Actually, you can't swim; you can only float. You can literally lay stretched out on top of the water due to the buoyancy. Imagine Superman flying through the skies and that's the picture of someone on top of the salty water of the Dead Sea.

So what does this have to do with anything? For me it is a picture of being abandoned to and for God. You see, the Sea of Galilee has water coming in one end and pouring out at another location. It constantly takes in the fresh water of the Jordan River, releasing life-giving water downstream. From there the water continues south to the Dead Sea, ceasing to give life. The reason? The Dead Sea has no outlet. The water sits there, consumed by itself. It's amazing to me that God would choose this land, knowing it contained so many life lessons for us.

Rivers of living water flow from the heart of those who believe in Jesus (John 7:38).

Living an abandoned life calls for us to share the refreshing water of God's Word to others in order to bring them life. We are to echo the love and blessings of God. This is one reason for the book you hold in your hand. Keeping the bitter waters of abandonment, rejection, and pain within us destroys the life and destiny God has for us. Our journey becomes nothing more than a sea of death. Your life was meant to be boldly poured out for others. You were designed to receive God's life and then release it for others.

"If you try to hang on to your life, you will lose it. But if you give up your life for my sake and for the sake of the Good News, you will save it" *(Mark 8:35).*

Give your life away for others!

Live abandoned!

Father! My prayer is that you would richly bless all those who have read this book! May they grow in their relationship with You. May they experience the joy of salvation and freedom that comes through relationship with You. May they discover their purpose and walk in their God-designed destiny. May each of them live abandoned for You! Amen.

CHAPTER FIFTEEN

TO BE CONTINUED...

Made in the USA
Columbia, SC
26 August 2019